Ecstasy

Its History and Lore

THIS IS A CARLTON BOOK

Design copyright © 2000 Carlton Books Limited
Text copyright © 2000 Carlton Books Limited

Pictures © various, see Picture Acknowledgements

This edition published by Carlton Books Limited 2000
20 Mortimer Street
London
W1N 7RD

A CIP catalogue for this book is available from the British Library.

ISBN 1 85868 862 0

Design: Adam Wright/bluefrog
Picture research: Deborah Fioravanti
Production: Garry Lewis

Ecstasy

Its History and Lore

Miriam Joseph

CARLTON
BOOKS

CONTENTS

PICTURE ACKNOWLEDGEMENTS

The publishers would like to thank the following sources for their kind permission to reproduce the pictures in this book:

Demon Imaging Ltd 30, 32, 57, 64, 66, 73, 75, 83

John Frost 80

PA News Photo Library 6/Sean Dempsdy 89

Pictorial Press Limited 60, 92

Topham Picture Point 36, 44

Science Photo Library/Prof. K. Seddon and Dr.T. Evans, Queens University Belfast 10/John Greim 46/Cordelia Molloy 25/Tek Image 9, 23

Every effort has been made to acknowledge correctly and contact the source and/or copyright holder of each picture, and Carlton Books Limited apologises for any unintentional errors or omissions which will be corrected in future editions of this book.

INTRODUCTION

Illicit drugs are one of the biggest leisure activities in the world today, representing an estimated US$400 billion per annum industry. During the twentieth century they moved, despite the best efforts of governments and law enforcers, from the underground into the mainstream. This series of books tells the stories of these drugs, from their initial synthesis and use as therapeutic or medical aids, to their adoption as adjutants to pleasure. It also tells of the increasingly draconian legislation attendant as each drug moved from the medical to the sybaritic world.

Ecstasy is the only drug that spawned a youth movement, rather than merely helping it on its way. Originally synthesized in 1912, it was used in therapy and as an aid to the terminally ill. *Ecstasy* charts the drug's move from the analyst's consulting room to the night-club and describes how, more than any other drug, ecstasy came to represent a generation.

INTRODUCING ECSTASY

Drop an "E" and wait for it to kick in – heart pounds, mouth dries, pupils dilate, the empathy trip begins – and you dance forever. "E" or "Ecstasy", is the drug that fuelled and helped construct an entire youth culture in the last decade of the second millennium. The term "Ecstasy" was coined well over twenty years ago to describe the overall experience of taking the drug 3,4-methylenedioxymethamphetamine (MDMA). Although Ecstasy is the most commonly used nickname for MDMA, it has been given various other street names, some of which sound as enticing as sweets in a confectionery shop. The list includes "Mickey", "Love Doves", "Rhapsody", "Biscuits" and "M&M's"; however, Ecstasy remains the most popular street name for MDMA, as the word most closely approximates the feelings the drug induces in the user.

WHAT IS IT?

Ecstasy is a hallucinogenic amphetamine. Put very simply, it has the combined characteristics of amphetamine ("speed") and LSD ("acid"). So, as well as stimulating the central nervous system (CNS), MDMA can also cause, on rare occasions, auditory and visual hallucinations, depending on the strength of the drug taken. But this is not a common effect of the drug. Because of the dual nature of its effects, MDMA is believed by many people, erroneously, to be a chemical blending of different drugs. In fact, MDMA is a synthesized substance with its own unique chemical makeup.

Most Ecstasy users say that the drug elicits feelings of love, euphoria and sensuality. Ecstasy today is typically taken at night-clubs, bars, cafes and at the very popular "raves". One writer has even described Ecstasy and the overall rave scene as *"a way of life"*. The effects of Ecstasy, as with any other drug, depend on the individual characteristics of the taker, but in the main, they include

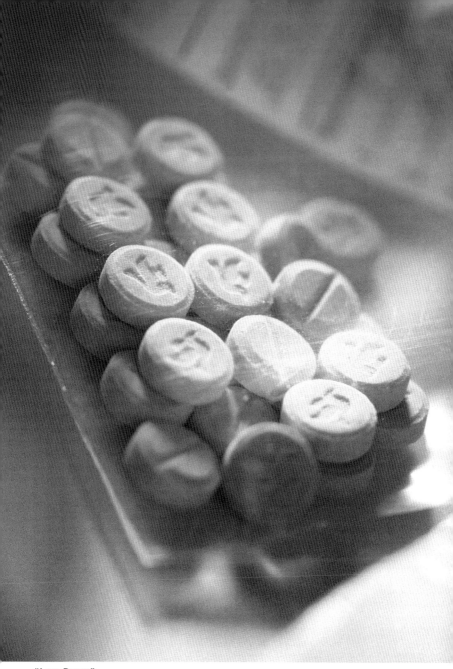

"Love Doves"

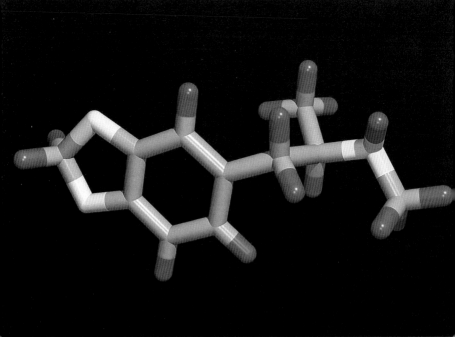

increased heart rate, feelings of general empathy with the world around you, a loss of inhibitions and a change in the quality of light-perception.

Because MDMA has several features that distinguish it from both amphetamines and the classic hallucinogens, newer terms have been suggested as being more appropriate for MDMA. "Empathogen" (short for empathy generating substance), a term coined by Dr Ralph Metzner, has been used to describe the effects that MDMA elicits. This term was proposed because the primary effects of MDMA are to cause an open emotional state and engender empathy or "sympathetic bonding" with others. Another term has been suggested by Dr David Nichols, who believes that MDMA does more than just elicit empathy. He coined the term "entactogen" because of the drugs ability to generate what he described as "touching from within".

Realistically, how one classifies MDMA is a matter of personal choice. What is obvious and apparent is that MDMA has a stimulating effect on the CNS in a majority of its users, while also inducing feelings that have been characterized as predominantly euphoric or blissful. In the main, MDMA has been available to users in the form of a white pill. But sometimes, especially in its early days, before manufacture became standardized, it could also be obtained as a white powder.

Many scientific and popular publications refer to MDMA as a "designer drug" but this is incorrect. Designer drugs are defined as *"variations of already controlled synthetic drugs which mimic the effects of the classical narcotics, stimulants and hallucinogens."* By this definition, MDMA does not qualify. This mistaken classification has given MDMA a stigma that it has never been able to shake off.

THE "DOWN" SIDE

While one person can take a certain drug and have a pleasurable experience, another person may take the same drug and dosage at the same time, in the same place and end up suffering irreversible damage or perhaps even a fatal reaction. The psychological make-up of each individual who takes Ecstasy plays an important part in his or her response to the drug.

There have been deaths among ecstasy users, yet the number is remarkably low considering that a sizeable proportion of the millions of people who to go out at weekends to a rave party or other event are using the drug. In fact, it is quite fortunate, yet surprising, that more deaths have not occurred, bearing in mind the wide range of adverse side-effects and physiological complications that have manifested themselves among the drug's users. The less serious unwanted side-effects of Ecstasy use can include chronic teeth-grinding, jaw-clenching, increased muscle tension, blurred vision and – the day after – a hangover that can cause fatigue, sleeplessness, sore jaw muscles, loss of balance and an aching head.

More disturbing is a phenomenon known as "head rush" – usually occurring at a rave where, for up to three minutes, dancers can experience a "blanking out" of all sights and sounds. Ecstasy can also act as an appetite-suppressant, so long-term users run the risk of suffering a range of problems associated with malnutrition. Some long-term users have reported an increased susceptibility to colds, flu, sore throats, and the like, suggesting that the drug (or the lifestyle that goes with it) suppresses the body's natural immunity to diseases. Research to date also suggests that Ecstasy can cause complications in people already suffering from heart disease, high blood pressure, glaucoma, epilepsy or who are generally in poor physical or mental health.

Some women who use Ecstasy report that their periods have been irregular and heavier than normal, while others say they have no periods at all when taking the drug. There is no evidence that MDMA damages a developing foetus or leads to problems in a newborn baby. However, the consensus view among physicians is that all drugs (licit and illicit) should be avoided during pregnancy, unless they are absolutely necessary for the management or treatment of a medical condition, and then only under medical supervision.

HEATSTROKE

Ecstasy causes a rise in body temperature. When the drug is taken in a hot, crowded environment such as a rave, and the consumer then dances frenetically for several hours, his or her body temperature can rise even more dramatically. Pints of fluid are lost through sweat and – in susceptible individuals – a fatal heatstroke can occur. Convulsions and widespread blood-clotting accompany the sudden rise in temperature and victims can go into a terminal coma. Between 1988 and October 1993, at least 14 such cases were reported in the UK. Why some people come to grief in this way, even on comparatively low doses, while others can withstand far more excessive use, remains a puzzle. Many Ecstasy deaths have been the result of blood clots forming in major blood vessels. This has most often occurred in the lungs, leading to respiratory collapse and death. It is believed that MDMA can precipitate this condition by somehow reacting with the chemicals that control the coagulation of the blood.

In October 1993, the Department of Medicine and Pharmacology at Sheffield University put forward a further possible explanation for this "sudden death syndrome" among some Ecstasy users. They suggested that the fatalities were linked to the absence of an enzyme called cytochrome P450246 in susceptible individuals. This enzyme is responsible for breaking down Ecstasy in the body. With the enzyme missing, so the theory went, the drug remains in the system long enough to cause fatal toxic effects. About one in twelve people were said to be missing this key enzyme – which still left open the question of why so few deaths when a million young people go raving every week, a good proportion of whom would have been popping Ecstasy pills? The team responsible for the theory admitted that a lot more work was needed on the subject.

EXCESS FLUID INTAKE

By now, most of those who go to clubs have got the message about reducing the risks of overheating by wearing loose clothes, "chilling out" regularly and drinking plenty of fluids. However, there have been at least three recorded deaths resulting from excessive fluid intake, possibly because of a mistaken belief that simply drinking lots of water will counteract the adverse side-effects of taking Ecstasy.

This condition is called dilutional hyponatremia – sometimes also known as "water intoxication".

Ecstasy appears to disrupt the normal functioning of the kidneys by causing the inappropriate secretion of an anti-diuretic hormone, which prevents the normal excretion of excess fluid. As a result, water is retained in the body, especially in the highly water-absorbent brain cells, causing the brain to swell. Eventually, the increased pressure on the brain shuts down vital functions such as breathing and heartbeat. Symptoms include dizziness and disorientation and, in severe cases, collapse and coma. Not all of those affected die; there have been a number of young people who have been admitted to hospital in this condition, but who have survived.

HEART FAILURE

Ecstasy causes a significant rise in blood pressure and heart rate, which a young, fit person can normally sustain. However, a few young people have succumbed to these stimulant effects, sometimes because of an undiagnosed heart condition. Many questions remain about Ecstasy fatalities. For example, the direct link between levels of the drug in the blood and its toxicity are unclear. The available US medical literature cites cases in which users with a normal dose of around 100–150mg of MDMA in their blood have died but others with a much higher level have survived. American psychiatrists have reported administering 100mg to patients during therapy with no ill effects whatsoever. Ecstasy deaths in the UK have involved a wide range of doses, anything from one to five or more tablets in one session.

LIVER DAMAGE

There is some evidence that Ecstasy may harm the liver, including reports of hepatitis (liver inflammation) and jaundice in users of the drug. Of more concern is a report published in *The Lancet* by a team at the National Poisons Unit, at Guy's Hospital, London, which described seven cases of severe liver damage associated with Ecstasy use. Most made a partial recovery, but one needed a liver transplant and another died. The authors of the article said that none of those affected had a history of heavy alcohol or intravenous drug use and none had signs of infectious hepatitis – factors that might otherwise have explained their condition. The team believed that such cases were increasing and *"may be related to repeated exposure to MDMA..."* But they also suggested that the damage could have been done by a contaminant or additive, rather than by the drug itself.

The same team published details of other Ecstasy-linked conditions and deaths, also in *The Lancet*, but in a subsequent issue of the same journal, an Oxford neurologist complained that the group had failed to say how often the drug was being used in these cases.

"*Without doing so,*" he wrote, "*one cannot determine if MDMA is any more dangerous than aspirin. For the public to make rational decisions about recreational drug use the incidence of death and serious morbidity needs to be known. When medical scientists allow their data to be uncritically used, they reduce the chances of more serious messages being listened to.*"

BRAIN DAMAGE

Fears of MDMA-linked brain haemorrhage were raised following a 1992 report of four such cases in Scotland – although speed as well Ecstasy was consumed by the victims. Three made a good recovery and one died. The authors of the report thought that as the four cases occurred in one cluster, impurities in the drug might have played a major role.

A greater controversy relates to MDMA's supposed capacity to damage those brain cells related to the production and transmission of a chemical messenger, or neurotransmitter, in the brain called serotonin. Although there are still large gaps in what is known about the function of serotonin and the system that processes it, it is widely believed to be responsible for the regulation of sleep, appetite, sexual functioning and mood.

The argument centres on the suitability of extrapolating results using laboratory animals to cover human MDMA users, the way in which neurotoxicity (brain poisoning) is defined, and the degree to which the neurochemical changes caused by exposure to MDMA might diminish over time. An additional problem is that the animals in the experiments were usually injected with the drug rather than being given it orally, the usual method of consumption in humans.

According to one medical sceptic, Marcus Rattray, from Guy's Hospital, Ecstasy damages the fibres of some brain cells but has little effect on the cell bodies themselves. And that, he believes, could mean that the cells have the ability to repair themselves. Rattray believes that "*It is too simplistic to say Ecstasy kills neurones.*"

Studies involving humans subsequently showed that one group of Ecstasy users appeared to have reduced levels of serotonin in the fluid bathing their brain cells. But, again, this reduction might be temporary and does not necessarily demonstrate brain damage – only the possibility of such brain damage. In personality tests, the group concerned were said to be "*less impulsive and hostile and showed greater constraint and control. These were all aspects of behaviour thought to be mediated by serotonin.*"

PSYCHOLOGICAL EFFECTS

Another Ecstasy researcher found similar mood changes as long ago as 1986. In a letter to the *British Medical Journal*, complaining that a senior British doctor had looked only for the bad news in his Ecstasy research, a New Mexico physician, Dr George Greer, noted that *"eighteen of my 29 subjects reported positive changes in mood after their sessions; 23 reported improved attitudes, such as toward self and life in general; 28 reported improvement in interpersonal relationships, and three of the five couples reported improvements in their working life; 14 reported diminished use of abusable substances (alcohol, marijuana, caffeine, tobacco, cocaine, LSD); 15 reported beneficial changes in their life goals; and all nine subjects with diagnosable psychiatric disorders reported considerable relief from their problems..."*

But such benefits, pharmaceutical history shows us, will probably be temporary, only to be followed by a "rebound" condition, wherein precisely the opposite effects to those desired are experienced. Speed initially seems to produce increased energy levels and confidence but ultimately leaves users exhausted and shaken. Tranquillizers sedate at first but then go on to produce great agitation. Heroin induces a pain-free, carefree condition but in the end delivers just the opposite.

"Set" and "setting" are often considered to be integral factors regarding the overall drug experience, including the manifestation of adverse after-effects. "Set" is the term used to describe the drug user's attitude and expectations prior to consuming a chemical substance and "setting" represents the physical surroundings, as well as the social situation that the person is in. As with LSD, whether the Ecstasy experience is good or bad often depends on the mood of the user when the drug is taken, what the user expects to happen, and the friendliness or otherwise of the other people present and the surroundings.

In moderate doses, most Ecstasy users report a mild euphoric "rush" followed by feelings of serenity and calmness and the complete dissipation of anger and hostility. Although the drug appears to stimulate empathy between users, there is no evidence that Ecstasy is an aphrodisiac; it tends to enhance the sensual experience of sex, rather than stimulate the desire for sexual activity or increase sexual excitement. Ecstasy also inhibits orgasm in men and women and may also inhibit penile erection.

At moderate dosages, there is a heightened perception of the surroundings but usually without the "psychedelic" visual distortions and illusions invariably associated with LSD. So, in most cases, Ecstasy tends to be mind-expanding rather than hallucinogenic. However, some sensitive individuals may experience visual imagery, particularly in "the mind's eye", when the eyes are closed, and hallucinations have been reported at higher dosages. One of the residual effects of Ecstasy, after a "run" of several days of drug use, may be flashbacks. This is also a well-documented after-effect of using LSD, where the LSD "trip" is briefly relived some time after the event, maybe even years later.

Most of the bad experiences with Ecstasy have been reported by those using higher doses over a period of time. They include anxiety, panic, confusion, insomnia, psychosis, and visual and auditory hallucinations. Generally, these effects will stop once the drug is stopped, but can leave the user in a weakened mental and physical condition for quite a while. There are already signs that some heavy Ecstasy users are suffering some very un-Ecstasy-like feelings: depression, loss of confidence, shakiness, anxiety – all of which may persist for varying lengths of time.

Manchester's Lifeline drug agency says in their *Ecstasy and Eve* booklet: *"We knew people who, once the life and soul of the party, were stuck in the house anxious, confused, tired and depressed... What had started out as the drug to end all drugs – the perfect drug – was leaving behind it a sorry catalogue of people in jail, people in mental hospitals, and shady people selling snidey drugs to eager young recruits looking to start on the honeymoon period. More and more reports came to Lifeline about long weekends brought to a close with a handful of Diazepam, Temazepam and even heroin. People who started taking drugs to make them feel good were having to take other drugs just to stop them feeling bad – sad!"*

It is the impact of Ecstasy on the emotional stability of young users which may prove its most important health legacy. The drug's capacity to strip some users of their psychological defences, to encourage them openly to trust and empathize, can prove costly in the long term. Whether the mechanism at work in the brain is psychological, neurological or just a factor of the communal rave culture is a question that's unlikely to be settled in the near future.

There has been some discussion in medical literature about the exact link between adverse psychological reactions and the use of a mind-altering substance. Some experts believe that such a drug, in and of itself, induces various adverse reactions, while others believe that the drug may simply exacerbate an established psychological or psychiatric condition or neurological abnormality that might otherwise never have appeared.

It remains entirely possible that drugs alone may trigger the onset of a wide range of adverse reactions or exacerbate pre-existing conditions. What is certain, however, is that drugs taken on the illicit market are unpredictable and worthy of some caution. For example, MDMA in its purest form can cause a wide range of reactions from minor and transient side-effects to death. Drugs sold on the illicit market are almost always adulterated and so are not in their purest form. One investigation into the adulteration of MDMA reported that, in tests on dozens of tablets sold as Ecstasy, many other ingredients were found to have been mixed in.

TOLERANCE AND ADDICTION

Inevitably, regular users develop a tolerance to the effects of Ecstasy so that they need increasing amounts to get high. While there are no major physical withdrawal symptoms associated with Ecstasy, of the sort experienced with heroin or barbiturates, depression, fatigue, anxiety and the like can follow cessation of use. This, of course, can lead to its continued and increased use in an attempt to alleviate these symptoms.

ECSTASY AND OTHER DRUGS

Mixing Ecstasy with alcohol, prescribed medications or drugs such as LSD, amphetamines, heroin or ketamine can have unpredictable and potentially dangerous results. Ketamine is a powerful anaesthetic, mainly given to child patients in hospital, which has found its way into the clubs in recent years. Medical text books warn of its potential for causing hallucinations and other "psychotic" outcomes, and that's precisely what the experience has been for recreational users. It produces hallucinogenic painkilling effects similar to those of PCP ("angel dust"), but is much shorter-lasting and probably less toxic. Ketamine also increases muscle tone, speeds up the heart and raises blood pressure.

Few who have tried ketamine, also called "Ketalar" or "special K", have many favourable words to say about it. It is available on the street in the form of powder, tablets, capsules, or liquid costing up to £20 for a single dose and can be taken orally, snorted or injected. Anaesthetics in general react especially badly with Ecstasy. If a person who has taken Ecstasy needs medical attention, especially when there is the likelihood that he or she will require surgery, it is very important that paramedics, doctors, dentists and other medical staff are informed about the person's use of the drug.

Ecstasy, and the dance culture that it has supported, has opened up a doorway to experimentation with a wide assortment of other substances. Western society has entered the twenty-first century as a poly-drug using society. No more the days when one drug was THE drug of the moment. Today anything goes. Young people are trying out a whole range of mind-altering drugs; old established drugs on the scene like LSD and speed and also newer drugs, such as ketamine and gammahydroxybutrate (GHB).

GHB was developed in the USA as a possible anaesthetic and premedicant for surgery, but authorization for its medical use was revoked in 1990 after certain undesirable side-effects started to appear. It is a salty tasting, colourless, odourless liquid that is supplied in small bottles. Apart from clubbers, the main users of GHB are body-builders who are attracted to its apparent ability to promote "slow-wave" sleep, during which a muscle-building growth hormone is secreted.

In clubs, this drug has been given all sorts of names including "Liquid E", "Liquid X", and even GBH (grievous bodily harm) to signify the potential "violence" of the drug experience. A bottle usually contains enough of the drug for three separate hits and costs up to £15. It is still available in the USA as a health food product and is promoted as an aid to sleep and weight-control at a recommended dose of around 2.5 grams. Although it isn't approved as a food or a drug in the UK, it is not currently restricted under the Misuse of Drugs Act. Possession is not illegal, but its unlicensed manufacture or distribution is an offence.

IN THE BEGINNING...

Ecstasy has a relatively short and easily traceable history. The drug is just one member of the 179-strong methylenedioxyamphetamine (MDA) family of chemicals. The story of Ecstasy begins in 1910 with the synthesis of its parent drug, MDA, by two German chemists. Not much happened on the MDA front until the late 1930s, when the drug was tested on animals during research into the stress hormone adrenaline (epinephrine in the USA). In 1941, MDA underwent trials as a possible treatment for Parkinson's disease, but was rejected when the trial subject complained of "increased rigidity". In 1957, Gordon Alles, a US chemist researching the therapeutic qualities of amphetamines, described to a scientific meeting MDA's potential for heightening perception and producing strange visual distortions. He had experimented with the drug several times and was speaking both from a scientific and personal point of view.

The story of MDMA, MDA's most famous offspring, followed a similar course. It was first synthesized in 1912 by the German pharmaceutical company E. Merck and Co. The original petition for the patent was made on Christmas Eve of 1913. Shortly thereafter, in 1914, the patent was issued to the company in Darmstadt, Germany. One of the most enduring myths about Ecstasy tells an unlikely tale, but a charming one. The story tells of a cease-fire in no man's land during the First World War, when British and German soldiers laid down their guns, climbed out of their trenches and played a friendly game of football together – of course they had all taken the newly invented MDMA!

Although small modifications were made to the drug in the following five years, it was never marketed. Just like MDA before it, MDMA was largely ignored for the next forty years. There is a popular misconception that MDMA was intended as an appetite suppressant, for the control of clinical obesity. In fact, its patent shows that MDMA was intended as a "precursor agent", deemed to contain primary constituents for other therapeutically active compounds. So MDMA was not developed as a dietary agent and nor was it ever used for such a purpose, although many writers have said as much. Even today, the claim that MDMA is an appetite suppressant continues to be erroneously reported in the lay press and even in some medical literature.

MDMA was investigated by Gordon Alles, the Californian drug researcher who had first described MDA, and then by a latter-day guru of Ecstasy, Dr Alexander T. Shulgin.

CHEMICAL WARFARE AGENT

When the American Office of Strategic Services (OSS) became the Central Intelligence Agency (CIA), its chemical division began a vast secret programme of research into the drug lysergic acid diethylamide 25 (LSD) under the more general rubric "non conventional agents", with the code-name Project MK-Ultra. LSD is an extremely powerful hallucinogenic. It was first synthesized in 1938 by Dr Albert Hoffman, a Swiss chemist. The very man who synthesized the drug was the first to experience the classic elements of an acid "trip". Quite by accident, Dr Hoffman ingested some LSD in 1943 while carrying out experimental work on the drug.

In his diary, he describes how he was soon overcome by *a remarkable but not unpleasant state of intoxication... characterized by an intense stimulation of the imagination and an altered state of awareness of the world. As I lay in a dazed condition with eyes closed there surged up from me a succession of fantastic, rapidly changing imagery of a striking reality and depth, alternating with a vivid, kaleidoscope play of colours.*

LSD was used in psychotherapy for many years but was made illegal in the USA and the UK in the 1960s when more and more people started taking it for casual recreational use without supervision. LSD in the 1960s, like Ecstasy in the 1990s, was the basis for a psychedelic revolution that changed youth culture forever.

The CIA's Project MK-Ultra was a huge undertaking, international in scope and uncompromising in nature. Guided by the general objectives of launching "surprise attacks" against "anti-American" elements, the US Government set up foundations and provided generous grants to several prominent scientists in order to investigate whether LSD was effective in:

- creating memory disturbances
- altering sexual habits
- eliciting secret information
- increasing suggestibility
- causing dependency.

Dr H. Abramson, a psychiatrist, was one of those given resources by the CIA in 1953 to research LSD and investigate its potential effects on the enemy. He finally had to tell the CIA that LSD wouldn't work for them because *"the effect is an essentially joyous disturbance of the ego function...Users generally enjoy the experience"*.

At around this time in the early 1950s, MDMA was also used in a series of animal experiments carried out with the support of the US Army. This was the first time that the substance had undergone really close scrutiny. Numerous tests were performed on non-human subjects including mice, rats, guinea-pigs, dogs and monkeys to assess the toxicity of MDMA. These experiments were called LD50 studies and were carried out to determine the approximate dosage of the substance needed to kill these animals, in order to establish an upper limit for its administration to humans (50 per cent of the lethal dose – or LD50).

By 1957, the American military added MDA and MDMA to the long list of substances that it was exploring as potential brainwashing and chemical warfare tools. As experimental agents, MDA was code-named EA1299 and MDMA was code-named EA1475. Fairly extensive trials were carried out on these two substances at the Edgewood Chemical Warfare Service (ECWS) in Maryland. The trials were principally intended to establish whether the two drugs could help to extract information from military prisoners and even immobilize enemy forces. MDMA was identified by the Edgewood Arsenal as one of the most toxic substances of those being investigated. But it was found to be less toxic than its parent drug MDA, a substance to which it has often been compared.

THE GURU OF ECSTASY

There has been much published in the scientific journals over the years about the effects that MDMA has on the chemical neurotransmitters that enable the brain and nervous system to function. Most of the laboratory studies involving the administration of MDMA have examined if, and to what degree, the substance has an effect on the brain's primary neurotransmitter, serotonin. The first person to publicly describe the effects of MDMA in humans was Dr Alexander Shulgin who published a very simple method of synthesis.

Born in 1925, the son of Russian *émigrés*, Shulgin served in the US Navy during the Second World War and then studied chemistry at university before deciding on a career in psychopharmacology. In 1960, he sampled mescaline, a hallucinogenic alkaloid from the peyote cactus, and discovered a vivid, wondrous world that would define the course of his future life. He wrote about his experience afterward, saying: *"I understood that the entire universe is contained in the mind and the spirit. We may not choose to find access to it, we may even deny its existence, but it is indeed there inside us, and there are chemicals that can catalyse its availability."*

Very soon after his mescaline experience, Shulgin took a job with the Dole Chemical Company and began to experiment with substances that resembled mescaline. Unlike other chemists, he measured their effects not on laboratory animals but on himself. This kind of behaviour, however productive Shulgin was, did not go down well with such a conservative company and by 1966 Shulgin had been forced to give notice. He set up his own laboratory at home in Lafayette, California, in a large outbuilding at the bottom of his garden. From here, Shulgin began to generate an inexorable stream of new mind-altering drugs for the next thirty years.

It was, and still continues to be, Dr Shulgin's fervent belief that psycho-pharmacological exploration can yield more useful tools to prise open the doors of perception in the human mind. He didn't see the point in testing his substances on laboratory mice or other animals – how would that give any indication of how these drugs affect the workings of the human brain? Instead, he gathered around him a group of people, including his own wife Ann, who would gladly ingest and experiment with all the new substances that he was producing in his garden laboratory.

These drug sessions were highly refined and enlightened events, where a group of friends would get together at someone's home, bringing food, drink and bedding for an overnight stay. They would take the drugs and do different things when the mood took them. They could talk, or listen to music, or walk, or cook, or couples could make love, or just sit around and read. Whatever they did, the agreement was that they would submit reports to Shulgin detailing the various effects the drug had had on them.

Soon, this bearded, jovial, exceedingly polite man, nicknamed "Sasha" by his friends, would become the figurehead of the new 1980s and 1990s psychedelic generation, just like Timothy Leary had been for the flower children of the 1960s. But unlike Leary, Shulgin, through his natural modesty and caution, doesn't particularly revel in this given role.

Many have asked the question, how was Shulgin allowed to carry on such research for so long? After all, he was making and taking endless numbers of psychoactive materials, which were either illegal already or about to be made illegal. The answer is that he had a Drug Enforcement Administration (DEA) licence to possess and analyse any drug he chose to. He was given this licence as his reward for being useful as an expert witness and consultant to the DEA. This situation could sometimes reach bizarre and even farcical proportions, especially when DEA officials picked up a new drug on the streets and brought it to Shulgin for analysis – only to discover that it was one of the substances that Shulgin himself had synthesized in his own back yard!

But Shulgin's independence could not last forever and, in 1994, DEA officials turned up with a warrant to search his premises. Shulgin was subsequently stripped of his licence and fined $25,000 – but this was by no means the end of the pharmacological quest that Shulgin had embarked on years before.

Shulgin had first synthesized MDMA at the Dole Company in 1965, but didn't actually try it on himself until late in 1967. Although he was an old hand at using various psychedelic substances and of their many and varied effects, he was astounded by the sensations he experienced with MDMA: *"I found it unlike anything I had taken before,"* he said. *"It was not a psychedelic in the visual or interpretative sense, but the lightness and warmth of a psychedelic was present and quite remarkable."*

In early 1977, Dr Shulgin introduced MDMA to Leo Zoff, an old friend and fellow psychologist. Zoff had already used LSD in therapy sessions during the 1960s and had found it useful in helping his patients to "open up" and communicate their feelings more effectively. By the late 1970s, Zoff was ready to retire from clinical practice, but he became obsessed with MDMA and began to travel around the USA introducing it to other psychologists and psychiatrists and extolling its therapeutic potential. It is estimated that Zoff convinced at least four thousand of his fellow professionals about the benefits of using MDMA and they, in turn, passed that wisdom on.

ECSTASY THERAPY

MDMA has been called an "empathogen" (empathy generating substance) to stress the difference between it and the other psychedelic substances available. Empathy is the sensation of experiencing someone else's feelings as your own, and this was the effect that Shulgin, and the

Highway to the mind's universe

many psychotherapists who followed his example, had celebrated. Successful psychotherapy can be defined as the attainment of common goals that have been set out by both the therapist and the client. The empathic component, or degree of compatibility, is an essential aspect of successful psychotherapy. For the therapy to be worthwhile, therapists must be able to establish a rapport and understanding with their clients.

MDMA, which was being administered only under the direction and guidance of attending psychotherapists, was believed to enhance this empathic understanding and to provide other sensory and spiritual benefits to those who sought help. Throughout the 1970s, psychotherapists all over the USA, who believed that the drug facilitated the healing process, were advocating MDMA-assisted psychotherapy.

The use of mind-penetrating compounds for the treatment of patients in psychiatry and psychotherapy had a long history that preceded MDMA's arrival on the scene. Various other substances, such as LSD, had already been used within the offices of psychotherapists and in psychiatric hospitals to enhance the overall psychotherapeutic process. Sometimes only the client would ingest the substance but on other occasions both client and therapist would take it. The following description sums up how many therapists viewed the benefits of psychoactive drugs:

"In the hallucinogenic experience, repressed memories flood forth in an emotional catharsis that leaves the once troubled person liberated from the core trauma from which his/her psyche suffered. Childhood memories are reactivated and relived with intense and extraordinary clarity accompanied by similar emotions. The flow of thoughts and feelings are so strong that they are difficult to repress."

During the 1970s and early 1980s, MDMA could be found on the shelves in the offices of numerous psychiatrists across America. MDMA was readily given to clients during therapeutic sessions as it had been deemed to be a catalyst that facilitated communication, heightened recognition and helped in the gaining of insight. This shimmering white powder, now widely recognized by its nickname Ecstasy, was being touted as the chemical key to enlightenment – with the capacity to enhance both self-understanding and empathy toward others.

Dr Shulgin released the first publication to discuss the pharmacological action of MDMA in the latter part of 1970. This report revealed that the substance elicits a controlled altered state, while also inducing feelings of sensuality or extreme gratification. The effective dosage taken by humans was determined to be 75–150mg when taken orally.

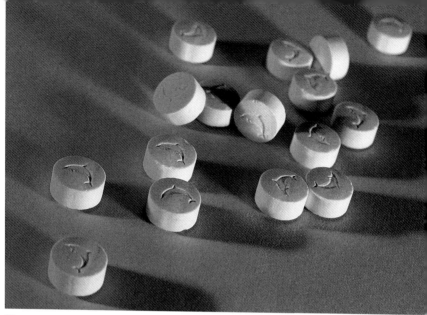

"I LOVE THE WORLD AND THE WORLD LOVES ME"

Dr George Greer, a long-time MDMA advocate, reported that the drug enabled people to communicate ideas, beliefs, opinions and memories that may have long been repressed in them. A similar paper, by Adamson and Metzner, explained that MDMA-assisted therapy had been utilized as a means of gaining access to the very memories that might otherwise have remained confined within the patient's psyche.

Dr Joseph Downing, a medical practitioner in favour of the use of MDMA in therapy, described the drug's effects as being characterized by a sense of well-being in which patients are able to deal with childhood trauma or other deeply repressed emotions. The use of MDMA seems to have combined different elements, including aiding relaxation and spiritual enlightenment, as well as facilitating the more traditional features of psychotherapy.

Some therapists in America believed that MDMA was a useful means of opening pathways of communication, as its use seemed to help individuals to overcome their inhibitions. Professionals in the mental health field reported that the MDMA-induced state enabled patients to resolve long-standing conflicts and inter-personal problems. Several of these accounts revealed that MDMA was a convenient way to help people reorganize their lives, and in that way enable them to deal with provoking memories, conflicts, and anxieties that might otherwise have remained hidden at an unconscious level.

The use of MDMA within therapy is best summed up by Rosenbaum and Doblin, as follows:

"MDMA encouraged the experience of emotions by reducing the fear response to perceived emotional threats. There were no direct observable harmful physical effects. For example, couples who were having marital problems were treated with MDMA-assisted psychotherapy, by psychiatrists and psychotherapists who believed that MDMA could facilitate communication. Trauma victims were treated with MDMA-assisted psychotherapy to help them delve into the sources of their problems, experiencing a healing catharsis, and subsequently function more effectively."

In the 1970s, marriage guidance counselling was one of the key areas in which MDMA was found to be of benefit. When the drug was given to battling partners in the middle of a marital crisis, it helped to dissipate their anger toward each other, encouraged empathy between them and enabled them to see each other's point of view. This allowed the two partners to talk without allowing their previously ever-present hostility to hinder their ability to communicate. The attending therapists of one particular study concluded that:

"Not only is communication enhanced during the session, but afterward as well. Once a therapeutically motivated person has experienced the lack of true risk involved in direct and open communication, it can be practised without the assistance of MDMA. This ability can not only help resolve existing conflicts, but can also prevent future ones from occurring due to unexpressed fears or misunderstandings."

MDMA was also used to help terminally ill patients deal with the pain of their illnesses. One woman described the value of MDMA in her life when it was used to help reduce the chronic pain her husband was suffering prior to his death from cancer:

"This drug can allow people to die well. They die well in the emotional arms of their families. They get reconciliation; they talk about things they normally would never talk about... It's not particularly addictive, and even a one-shot deal would be marvellous for these people to go home after Uncle Joe dies and say, 'Gee, at least I told him I loved him,' and things like that. I think it's so sad that we don't have this in every hospital, not just for cancer patients, though I think it allows people to rise above their pain, too... My husband died at home in his bed... But because the MDMA had opened his psychic door, I was able to put him in this deep, trance-like state, so he was in great joy without the body."

For those who have endured a painful illness or have observed a loved one slowly die in agonizing pain, the idea of taking or giving a loved one a mood-altering drug to enhance the last few weeks of his or her life seems very appealing. With euthanasia and the "right to die movement" very much in the news, many people have openly expressed their views on this issue. Much has been written about the plight of terminally ill patients and the roles of both the medical staff and the family. For several years, professionals and lay people have openly campaigned for the right to administer mind-altering substances to those suffering from painful terminal illness. Now, many more people are coming to feel that psychoactive drugs should be given to patients on the basis of mutual consent by all three parties concerned – patient, family and doctor.

During the 1970s and early 1980s, a number of articles on MDMA appeared in the psychiatric literature and the popular press, most of which were highly favourable in their conclusions about the drug's benefits. The various uses that drugs like MDMA were being put to led US researcher Dr David Nichols to argue that the effects of drugs at the milder end of the MDA potency scale, such as MDMA, were different enough from amphetamine and from LSD and the other hallucinogenic drugs to warrant having a category all to themselves – "entactogens". This was part of an attempt by therapists and researchers to differentiate MDMA from other, more "disreputable" substances.

ECSTASY RISING

Inevitably, like LSD before it, Ecstasy leaked out on to the streets of the USA, taken mainly by middle-class professionals in search of some kind of "transcendental experience". People had started using Ecstasy from the late 1960s onward. Small exclusive groups were involved who wanted to keep it their "little secret". This worked for a while, but with the increasing popularity of Ecstasy in psychotherapy during the 1970s, word soon got around. In an almost identical manner to that of the early users of LSD, these Ecstasy adepts were very enthusiastic about their drug and were soon telling their friends all about it. These friends told other friends and so on, until interest in the drug began to snowball. Ecstasy was out of the bag and had hit the streets.

As with the first makers of LSD in California, the first mass-producers of MDMA in the early 1980s were of the elitist, therapeutic school. They were known as the "Boston Group". They made and supplied the drug out of a real belief in the drug's potential for helping and curing people and enhancing their lives. They would supply Ecstasy to users with "flight manuals" – instructions on how best to enjoy the trip, such as where to use the drug, what to drink and what not to drink, and how to negotiate the "comedown". This was not just an unusual gimmick, it showed that the first manufacturers of

Ecstasy expressed a healthy respect for the drug itself and demonstrated a concern for the health of their clients.

Central to the belief of this group was the necessity for the right "set" and "setting", ensuring a safe and stable atmosphere in which to take this powerful drug, thereby "programming" the trip for the best possible outcome. But all this soon changed. By the 1980s, a different group of people were using Ecstasy and for very different reasons. The so far well-preserved and safe Ecstasy cocoon had been broken.

By 1983, one renegade member of the Boston Group recognized the potential for making gargantuan profits out of this still legal drug that everybody seemed to want to get their hands on. With the backing of very rich and enthusiastic friends in Texas, he launched his own cartel – the "Texas Group". This group promoted Ecstasy aggressively, making it easily available in bars and clubs all over the state. Consequently, the first reports of sizeable non-therapeutic use of Ecstasy came from this state.

Reports out of Dallas, Texas, suggested that people entering clubs and bars not only bought their Ecstasy with hard cash but often paid with credit cards. This was an innovation brought in by the Texas Group – they even set up telephone hotlines so people could get their Ecstasy more easily and quickly. Club owners and those tending bars were said to have received these customers warmly, as Ecstasy was an easy and popular sale for them. The Texas Group claimed that Ecstasy was a "fun drug" and that it was "good to dance to".

The therapeutic fraternity was astounded and outraged. MDMA wasn't some Saturday night party drug, they claimed, it was a serious tool in psychological study. As far as the Boston Group was concerned, the Texas Group had become an organized drug-dealing gang rather than altruistic facilitators of happiness. As one Bostonian put it: *"Our perception of them was that they were primarily capitalists and that it's too bad they didn't take the drug more and a little longer before they embarked on their project... If they hadn't been on the scene, we probably could have sold it for another ten years."*

It is difficult to say exactly how much Ecstasy the Texas Group was manufacturing and selling. US estimates range from tens of thousands to millions of doses, tableted and sold in tiny brown bottles with the label, "Sassafras" on them. This label listed completely fictitious ingredients in order to pull the wool over the eyes of law enforcers by making them think that it was a health food product.

As Ecstasy was still a legal substance, it was easy enough for people to get their hands on it. One small Californian laboratory alone produced ten thousand doses a month in 1976, thirty thousand a month in 1984 and fifty thousand a month in 1985! Many of those using it in California were already familiar with the hallucinogenic effects of LSD – but Ecstasy had one up on LSD. It was also an amphetamine that could give them the energy to dance all night if they wanted to. This additional charge that Ecstasy provides made it a very popular drug on the dance scene in the USA.

THE CLUB DRUG

Texas and California were only two of many states where Ecstasy was being used as a dance drug – the black gay scene in other cities was fuelled by Ecstasy – but it was in these two states that the Ecstasy phenomenon seemed most widespread and best documented, as it was mostly clean-cut, white college kids who were taking the drug. The August 1985 issue of *Life* magazine ran a picture that was most telling: a girl clutching her head, dancing enthusiastically, her T-shirt hitched up around her torso with the bold letters XTC emblazoned on it. MDMA was gradually shedding its chemical name and its therapeutic concept and was taking on a totally new function – the pursuit of hedonism.

By the mid 1980s, Chicago and New York had become homes to a new music called "House" or "Garage" – a DJ-concocted genre that combined synthesized percussion tracks, high-energy sounds and selections from early 1980s soul and disco tracks. This was music to dance to – it was a sound that expected serious energetic dancing. The name "House" was derived from a club called the Warehouse, in Chicago, and "Garage" from the Paradise Garage club in New York, where much of the musical experimentation was carried out. Soon, DJs were going into recording studios to produce their own dance tracks and were making it in to the national music charts. The sounds and success soon crossed the Atlantic to the UK.

Already well used to absorbing the underground musical sounds of the USA, the north-west of England readily accepted House music and it filtered into clubs such as the Hacienda in Manchester. Opened in 1982 and owned by Tony Wilson, maverick boss of the legendary independent ("indie") record label, "Factory", the Hacienda was to become the crucible for the rave phenomenon to come. A second source for the revitalization of the UK club scene in the 1980s also came from outside the UK – the Mediterranean island of Ibiza.

A hippie hideaway of very long standing, Ibiza developed its own dance culture based on the sounds of House and Garage – but recast this as the "Balearic sound". Members of London's smart set and vacationers from the surrounding suburban working class areas, for whom Ibiza was a sunny holiday retreat, returned from the island with tales of the "beautiful fun" to be had. Under the high-energy influence

BALEARIC BEAT

of Ecstasy, the crowd partied for days at a time in what came to be known as the "Summer of Love" in 1987. The Ibiza mood was brought back to the clubs in London and from there spread out to the rest of England.

All the right places began filling up with young people of every size, shape, colour and disposition. They brought with them a new style of dressing down that included T-shirts, headbands, smiley symbols, hippie flares and even caftans. The mood was overwhelmingly peaceful and co-operative. Even the DJs were hugged – as opposed to ignored, which had been the case until then. This was the beginning of the cult of the DJ which, within five years, would elevate the most successful ones to the status of very famous and wealthy pop icons.

There has been a long association in the UK between all-night dancing and stimulant drug use dating back to the pre-war West End scene and its link with cocaine and the post-war West End scene of mods and speed. Both the American and Mediterranean music fashions, twinned with Ecstasy, spawned a dance scene in the UK that became the defining feature of British youth culture in the 1990s.

ECSTASY CENTRE STAGE

Much like LSD, twenty years before, the significance of Ecstasy to the rave phenomenon arose from its specific, identifiable pharmacological effects, which united the fans in a kind of collective esoteric rite. Technological advances in music had continued throughout the 1980s until, by 1987, the previously rigid boundaries between musical production and musical consumption were beginning to break down.

Firmly at the centre of this musical development was a brand new role for the club DJ. Unlike his traditional British counterpart, the Balearic DJ didn't merely play one record after another, interspersing the mix with inane chatter on the microphone. He was required to mix two or three records together, creating a distinctive collage of sounds and rhythms. With an extraordinary degree of manual dexterity, the best DJs would perform all manner of turntable tricks, turning a box of records into more than just the sum of its parts, providing a complex soundtrack for a whole night of dancing.

While making their new music, Ecstasy-using musicians began to pay particularly close attention to a special phenomenon of the drug – its ability to encourage repetitive behaviour. Many of the new Ecstasy evangelists suggested that, along with breaking down barriers in society, Ecstasy had led to the discovery of certain receptors in the brain that, when stimulated, make human beings want to dance.

Either the DJs had found a music that exactly matched the drug of the moment or a drug had surfaced that fitted the current musical trend, like a hand fits a glove. Slowly but surely, the Balearic spirit was left behind. Out went the hip-hop influences in the music and any rock influences that might disrupt the repetitive beat. The way Ecstasy engendered repetitive behaviour was a godsend to the DJs – they began to play versions of well-sequenced British House beats, liberating their music from the stifling restrictions so prevalent before. Soon, dance floors were full of people whose bodies seemed totally synchronized to the new music.

The other unique property of Ecstasy is that it acts as an empathogen, encouraging the user to understand and enter into the feelings of others. As a result of this twist, rave culture developed an emotional intensity it had never had before. Where the audience would normally face forward at concerts, venerating the live band and lead singer, they began to turn to each other and indulge in Ecstasy-inspired embraces. The scene even coined a make-shift verb – "loved up" or "luvved up" – to describe the intense emotional bonds formed

HI-TECH PLEASURE PRINCIPLE

by Ecstasy-consuming dancers toward total strangers. Ecstasy seemed to have removed the divide between the audience and the star. Ecstasy's empathogenic qualities also prompted the suggestion that it could and would irrevocably alter the consciousness of British youth culture.

A key element of the early days of rave was Ecstasy's apparent ability to break down rigid class, gender and race barriers and boundaries. Rave was a revolt against the heavily stylized and posed dress code of the 1980s and against the rigidity and elitism of many London clubs. Out went the "smart-casual" dress style of the Friday night clubber and in came the truly casual dresser, in gear that had previously only been worn by black hip-hopsters or championed by a soccer-supporting urban under-class.

The Manchester group Happy Mondays adopted a "baggy" style of clothing that they had borrowed from these groups. All of a sudden, most clubbers in the UK were dressing like that. A look involving loose trousers, T-shirts and floppy hats became *de rigeur* as it excluded no one – black or white, male or female, rich or poor.

Clubs were no longer places you went to to be part of the ubiquitous Saturday night, sexual-partner hunt. In a conscious rejection of overt sexuality, young people were giving out the message – dress not to impress but simply to have a good time.

Rave, according to one female commentator, allowed *"young women to occupy their social space with confidence"*. Many of the clubbers she spoke to reported a sense of joy and belonging and of feeling free of sexual threats. This fact also obliged many workers in the drug field to abandon the tired old stereotype of young women caught up in a male-dominated drug-taking world and becoming either victims or sexual deviants. She reported that the dance drug culture *"offers a view of women as active participants in drug use, instead of the more usual image of passivity and powerlessness."*

ECSTASY EVANGELISM

For those intent upon spreading the word about Ecstasy, the next obvious step was to make music that overtly eulogized and encouraged the use of the drug. For them, the 12-inch independent white label records were ideal, as they could be made up by individuals, sold in small numbers to record shops or even out of the back of a van and thus could get past the usual moral regulators; the record companies and the Government. There was a rash of such music right through 1989 and into 1990. One classic example was a track made by a Liverpool band called Mind, Body and Soul. They took a version of Jefferson Airplane's "White Rabbit", sampled the acid guru, Timothy Leary's clarion call, *"Turn On, Tune In, and Drop Out"* simply prefacing it with a voice that just said "Ecstasy"!

The comparisons that were made about the music and the culture were obvious – the second psychedelic wave was upon Britain. As it had been in the 1960s with LSD, it would be the job of musicians and like-minded people to go forth and proclaim the truth of this drug to the world. Writing in 1967, Timothy Leary, who had always emphasized the importance of musicians when it came to spreading the word, said: *"I've dropped out completely myself. I'm already an anachronism in the LSD movement anyway. The Beatles have taken my place"*. Leary even renamed the Beatles "The Four Evangelists".

For many bands in the UK in the 1990s, the 1960s were alive and well and the lesson to be learnt was an easy one – drop an Ecstasy tablet and everything would be all right. In 1990, Northside, a Manchester-based band signed to Tony Wilson's Factory Records, brought out a song called "Shall We Take a Trip". Through the song's lyrics, the band was making a direct connection with the 1960s psychedelic revolution.

As well as the boss of Factory Records, Tony Wilson was part-owner of the Hacienda club. Talking to the assembly at the New Music Seminar in New York in 1990, he tried to explain the grip that Ecstasy was beginning to have on the new British music scene:

"If you're a rock group and you cannot play rock music in the style to which you can dance and with the rhythms that have come out of America, but have been ignored here, then you aren't a rock group that matters... I went into my club, The Hacienda, two weeks ago and one-and-a-half thousand 18-year-old kids were going mental, dancing like crazy to Northside, to Mondays, to Marshall Jefferson, to Derrick May, to Pink Floyd, to the Beatles... I've never seen anything like it in my life and I felt old for the first time. The wave is that strong."

Though the clean and happy nature of the collective Ecstasy high was slowly beginning to wear off – it was far from over. The beat continued into 1992. Ecstasy consumption went up and more and more dance records contained lyrics encouraging people to partake in the Ecstasy experience. The Shamen's "Ebeneezer Goode" is a perfect example of a track that referred directly to Ecstasy, but whose lyrics were oblique enough to go uncensored. The song was a patent eulogy to the Ecstasy effect in livening up people and parties:

> *He takes you for a ride, and as if by design*
> *The party ignites like he's coming alive*
> *He takes you to the top, shakes you all around and back down...*
> [chorus] *Eezer Goode, Eezer Goode, he's Ebeneezer Goode.*

No more was Ecstasy the sole preserve of a small bohemian elite – it had been totally democratized to include even the most commercial of clubs. The summer of 1992 saw Mecca and Roxy discos all around the country echoing to the sound of entire dance floors singing *"Es are good, Es are good"* to the chorus of The Shamen's number one hit.

Ecstasy had become as essential to the dance scene as the music itself. Home Office statistics suggest that 1.5 million Ecstasy tablets were being consumed every weekend in 1995! Many surveys carried out into drug consumption among young people at that time showed that a considerable number of 14–20 year olds were taking drugs and that an even larger number had been offered them. This trend did not go unnoticed by the press, with *The Guardian* correctly interpreting this development as meaning that *"drug taking has become an integral part of youth culture"*.

THE ECSTASY CRUSADES

In the USA, an exuberant new drug scene was unlikely to go unnoticed by the authorities for long. As Ecstasy's star rose through the 1980s, the media began to pay more attention to it. The publicity that Ecstasy received in the American press was initially positive and tended to focus on what they called "the yuppie psychedelic", but that soon changed. What started out as a few isolated articles soon ballooned into a torrent of newsprint from newspapers and magazines all over the country. Soon, the Drug Enforcement Administration (DEA) started to take action. This was nothing out of the ordinary in a country where the President, Ronald Reagan, had already authorized and sanctioned a "war on drugs".

A crusade was launched to exorcise alleged demons of "otherness" from the American nation. Ecstasy had hit its first hurdle. However, a collective of MDMA supporters proposed that any action by the DEA should first be subject to a hearing, so that the therapeutic potential of Ecstasy was not lost to the medical community. In the prevailing mood under Reagan at the time, the idea that a mind-altering drug could be beneficial to people was shocking and outrageous. The struggle between the two camps intensified, but the DEA refused to give ground. The fact that Ecstasy might help a few people was a subtlety lost on those who had made a career out of the slogan "just say no". After all, Nancy Reagan was in the White House and the anti-drugs campaign was her personal crusade.

THE AMERICAN CRACKDOWN

In 1984, a US Senator from Texas, Lloyd Bentsen, made a formal request to the Drug Enforcement Agency to ban the drug Ecstasy. The first notice indicated that the proposed action was not only to make the drug illegal, but also to place it in the strictest of all drug

CRUSADER IN THE WHITE HOUSE

classifications – Schedule I. This sparked off a two-year debate over MDMA involving oral and written testimony.

In response to this first notice, and much to the surprise of law enforcement officials and the DEA, many interested professors, psychiatrists and physicians came forward in strong opposition to the proposed scheduling of Ecstasy. These advocates were opposed to the ruling because it would ultimately halt MDMA-assisted therapy and disrupt any continued research endeavours. They were driven by a firm belief that MDMA could be administered with safety within the realm of therapy provided its use was closely monitored. This contradicted the DEA view that MDMA had no accepted medical validity, regardless of whether there was professional supervision. However, the medical community's representations to the US Government on the value of MDMA as a therapeutic tool in counselling could not prevent the drug being banned.

In early 1985, preliminary hearings into the proposed scheduling of Ecstasy took place before the Administrative Law Judge. Further hearings were due to take place in California, Missouri and Washington, DC. On July 1 of that year, the administrator of the DEA used his emergency powers to place Ecstasy in Schedule I of the Controlled Substance Act (CSA) on a temporary basis. He said he believed there was a potential for dangerous misuse of the drug and so Ecstasy was to remain in this Schedule I classification until a more concrete ruling was made. This ruling would be based on courtroom proceedings with the testimonies of witnesses for both parties – pro and anti. Numerous further hearings took place in 1985 and 1986. A final ruling was given that placed Ecstasy in Schedule I of the CSA permanently, effective from November 13, 1986. This outlawed the drug totally. As a result, nobody can legally manufacture, sell or use it for any purpose whatsoever.

ILLICIT MANUFACTURE

The prolific Texas Group stepped up their production in advance of the impending criminalization of Ecstasy. Their Ecstasy factory went into overdrive, reportedly turning out over two million tablets as users stockpiled their supplies. In the months after criminalization, some of these entrepreneurs retired with their millions but many of them continued making and selling Ecstasy illegally. The lure of millions of dollars in profits was not so easy to give up after all.

Drug profits have always been able to dazzle, from the smallest of small-time back-alley dealers to the biggest of international traffickers. Many have said that the pull of drug money is sometimes stronger than the pull of the drug itself. Despite all the prohibitive laws and the vigorous activities of police and customs officers, drugs remain easily accessible to anyone who desires them only because illicit drug manufacturers are willing to run the gauntlet and take the risks involved, as they know that the potential rewards are far greater than the risks.

Although the clandestine manufacture and illicit supply of Ecstasy dates back only to the mid 1980s, by the end of that decade, the number of Ecstasy producing laboratories being detected each year began to reach a significant figure. This rapid development of the illicit Ecstasy market has been supported by a number of quite specific characteristics:

- Economies of scale play a large part in the profitability of Ecstasy production – small quantities of Ecstasy are not cost effective. To be as profitable as possible, Ecstasy must be manufactured on a large scale.
- Ecstasy manufacturing sites tend to be relatively near to the markets they serve, which reduces the subsequent risks involved in trafficking these drugs. This is in marked contrast to traditional plant-based narcotic drugs, such as heroin or cocaine, that are often produced far away from the end-user countries.
- It is difficult for the authorities to estimate the extent of synthetic drug manufacture, as the precursor materials needed for the process have, in the past, been much more easily and widely available than was the case with plant-based drugs and are rarely tied to a particular geographical area. With heroin and cocaine especially, governments and drug enforcement agencies have been able to build up a comprehensive database over the years, based on a study of the areas where the drug plants are cultivated.

Such economic factors have played an important part in determining the pace and direction of expansion of the manufacturing, trafficking and consumption of Ecstasy. The demand for Ecstasy is currently very strong and is close to topping that for both heroin and cocaine. Although economic factors cannot fully explain or predict future developments in the illicit drug market, they are key factors in influencing the behaviour of the main characters concerned with manufacture and supply.

It is the rule of any market that demand and supply go hand in hand. A producer can artificially increase demand for a product, but that demand cannot be sustained for too long on just a slogan or on the back of large stocks. Drug use is on the rise because people want to consume drugs for a variety of reasons and, in turn, suppliers have succeeded in accommodating their particular appetites. Like the pharmaceutical business, the trade in illicit drugs is also a global commercial enterprise, yet it is much more complex and dynamic because the producers must constantly outwit a vast enforcement effort specifically designed to thwart them.

Ecstasy laboratories are, on average, larger and require more sophisticated equipment and technologies than other laboratories that manufacture synthetic drugs. As with all other illicit synthetic drug manufacture, the drug is made in, or close to, the country of final consumption. Profit margins are particularly high at the manufacturing level, because highly specialized knowledge is required to make Ecstasy, which limits the number of people who can muscle in on production, yet the input prices are relatively low – certainly not as high as for crack cocaine – because the raw materials are cheaper and easier to obtain. Ecstasy generates higher profits per kilogram than does crack cocaine.

The profitability of Ecstasy trafficking is less clearly identifiable – although it appears to have been increasing in recent years in individual countries. There is little evidence that the finished product is moved around much, but the chemical precursors of Ecstasy are being trafficked in increasingly huge quantities. Due to the rising prices of precursor materials and the increasing difficulty in getting them, overall Ecstasy profits have fallen, from a few million per cent to several thousand per cent. However, the fall has not yet been enough to remove the sheer economic incentives that drive the expansion of illicit Ecstasy manufacture. In fact, when calculating the total gross profits from both producing and trafficking the drug, Ecstasy may be the most economically attractive illicit substance to make and distribute of them all.

As with any other drug, Ecstasy manufacturing started small and grew. Fifteen years ago, the manufacture of Ecstasy was a small-scale industry, with laboratories set up primarily in homes or small-scale outfits. Manufacturers have moved from the kitchen sink or bathtub to vast chemical laboratories. Today, Ecstasy laboratories are

INVISIBLE ECONOMY – A BATCH OF CONFISCATED DRUGS

overwhelmingly run by Mexican poly-drug trafficking organizations – any drug will do, as long as it makes a good profit. These outfits are controlled by drug manufacturers who both make and distribute the drug. Better organized, better funded, better equipped and much more resolute about their occupation and its phenomenal profits than a small-time drug producer, these organizations are ready for almost any eventuality. Having radically extended their production capabilities, they have virtually inundated the US market with Ecstasy.

Among those who were originally using Ecstasy in the USA were a whole range of quasi-mystical groups who had sprung up after the hippie era. One of the most successful of these groups was the Osho community. Its charismatic leader, Bhagwan Shree Rajneesh wasn't above amassing material – as well as spiritual – wealth. Although the various communes that he set up – 600 of them world-wide – were meant to have a strict no-drugs policy, some of the Bhagwan's followers, including former therapists, used Ecstasy among themselves. In the book, *Bhagwan – The God that Failed*, an early disciple and bodyguard of Rajneesh suggests that *"the euphoric, mood-altering drug Ecstasy was discreetly slipped into rich sanyassin's drinks just before fund-raising interviews."*

The fact that the Osho movement was outward-looking and entrepreneurial, rather than isolated, meant that the people who gravitated to it would not only popularize Ecstasy, but would also put in place distribution systems that would take Ecstasy far beyond the USA. According to a book about Ecstasy in the Netherlands during the mid 1980s, Dutch followers of the Bhagwan were taking so much Ecstasy that many different supply lines were necessary to meet the growing demand. Before long, large-scale illicit manufacturers had established production centres in the Netherlands, Belgium, Germany, the UK, Spain and eventually even in some of the breakaway states of the former Soviet Union.

EUROPEAN TAKE-OVER

Although Ecstasy started its street life in the USA – Europe has gradually taken over as the main region for both production and consumption of the drug. Information presented in the document *Global Illicit Drug Trends – 1999* produced by the United Nations Office for Drug Control and Crime Prevention (ODCCP) highlights this change. Between 1985 and 1990, North America annually produced 49 per cent of the world's Ecstasy-type substances – but between 1991 and 1997 this figure dropped to just 30 per cent.

This downturn has been quite remarkable – and is due primarily to the increase in use and manufacture of the drug in Europe, and not to increased law enforcement pressure in the USA. Data from 1992 shows that the number of Ecstasy doses seized in the UK was over 550,000, compared with about 365,000 in the year before, a rise of more than 50 per cent. These figures from the UK show that Ecstasy taking was already almost as widespread as that of speed and much larger than that of either heroin or cocaine.

With Ecstasy use so widespread in Europe, a corresponding manufacturing industry was working hard to meet the demand. Many of the manufacturers of other drugs caught on pretty quickly and jumped on the Ecstasy bandwagon. It was easiest for those already established in the drug business to expand and incorporate a new and profitable product.

DOORKEEPERS AND THEIR FRIENDS

There is a widespread misconception that the criminal underworld in the UK was never interested in the drugs trade – that they felt it was a dirty business and wouldn't get involved. This may well have been true forty or fifty years ago – but is about as far from the truth today as saying young people don't take drugs. It would be fair to say that the definition of "dirty business" has changed over the years, especially given the amount of money that can be made from the drug trade.

Bernard O'Mahoney (alias Patrick Mahoney, alias, Bernie King) throws some light on the involvement of the underworld in his surprisingly candid and enlightening autobiography, *So This is Ecstasy*. O'Mahoney was the head doorman at a dance club called Raquels, in Basildon. The door-staff at Raquels were part of a gang that controlled drug dealing in numerous venues around Essex, Suffolk and south London. As well as straightforward drug dealing, O'Mahoney alleges that they stole drugs from other gangs, extorted protection money, carried out punishment beatings and enforced debt collection.

All of these activities were conducted with whatever level of intimidation and violence was considered necessary. Most of the gang members were well-armed with an astonishing variety of weapons ranging from knives to ammonia sprays, handguns and machetes – and were not backward about using any of them. They also enjoyed taking the drugs they were helping to distribute.

Just a few months after a teenage girl called Leah Betts died after taking an Ecstasy tablet in 1991, *Mixmag* magazine published an interview with Detective Chief Superintendent Anthony White of the Metropolitan Police, who was trying to get across to Ecstasy users exactly who was profiting from their pleasure:

"Ecstasy is a mass-produced drug, and the people who produce it and traffic it are extremely high up in the criminal hierarchy. They don't look

like clubbers, they don't look like the lead singer of The Prodigy, they look like me. They're big, violent, sad old gits, they're scumballs. They have no view on drugs other than making a profit out of them."

Rogue dealers who tried to sell drugs in any of the gang's clubs would soon have their money and their drugs confiscated and also ran the risk of getting beaten up. The confiscated drugs were sold on and the money was just an added bonus. Club managements had very little option but to turn a blind eye to the gang's activities. O'Mahoney explains it this way:

"They knew it was the drug culture that was filling their club to capacity. They were hardly going to root out the very thing that caused this new interest. It's the same story all over the country with rave clubs: what else do people think kids do in a club for eight to ten hours where there's no alcohol on sale?"

As the gang's activities became more widespread and more profitable, their drug intake also accelerated. O'Mahoney also had links with many other London gangsters, robbers and even the infamous convicted murderers of the 1960s, the Kray twins. His book put many of the myths about Ecstasy culture into harsh perspective. Organized crime wasn't just interested in Ecstasy, by now it had become synonymous with the Ecstasy trade. According to studies conducted by the influential market research and analysis organization, the Henley Centre for Forecasting, by 1993 at least £15 million was being spent on drugs every week. Needless to say, the profit margins in the Ecstasy trade were huge and therefore very lucrative for the gangs involved.

CHEMICAL CRUSADERS

In an interview conducted with a small group of Ecstasy producers in the UK, writer Nicholas Saunders found that they had started out in the business simply because they liked the drug. Once they decided to get into production, they spent a long time researching their subject, collecting information, obtaining equipment and buying the precursor materials. For the most detailed information about the synthesis of the drug, they studied chemistry textbooks, the works of Alexander Shulgin, the Internet, anything that might provide the data they needed.

Obtaining equipment was a more complicated matter, as this could quickly arouse suspicions if they were not careful, so they had to think laterally about the best places to look. Some of the unlikely locations they eventually turned to for their laboratory glassware included car boot sales and even theatre prop shops. The precursor materials were a little more difficult to get their hands on. Anyone attempting to buy these chemicals would be tracked down immediately. Some ingredients, such as Safrole, had to be obtained from black market sources at very high prices. They travelled abroad to buy some of the materials and those that they couldn't obtain, they had to make themselves, which turned out to be a very expensive process.

When Nicholas Saunders interviewed them, the young entrepreneurs said that the most difficult part of their enterprise had been the distribution. They didn't have an already established route, so they found it difficult to get rid of the large numbers of Ecstasy tablets they produced. As none of the manufacturers wanted to become full-time dealers, they spent some time devising an efficient distribution network so that they could then concentrate solely on the manufacturing. The other major lesson they learnt was that economies of scale are very important in the production of Ecstasy. To be really profitable, the drug should ideally be produced in large batches.

ESCALATING NUMBERS

Police figures detailing the amount of the drug being seized tends to back up the widespread view that there has been a massive increase in the illicit manufacture of Ecstasy in Europe. In fact, European output accounts for more than half the total global figure and is larger than that of speed production. Currently, the countries with the largest seizures of illicit Ecstasy are the UK, Germany, Spain and the Netherlands. There are also indications that Ecstasy is being trafficked from Europe to several rapidly developing areas in the Far East where it is being used in holiday and tourist resorts, primarily by European travellers but increasingly by the local inhabitants.

One result of the phenomenal demand for Ecstasy in the UK has been the increasingly professional nature of its supply. In the late 1980s, Ecstasy production was a relatively expensive process and very little production was actually being carried out in the UK, but by the early 1990s European and British Ecstasy laboratories had become highly commercial drug factories pumping out more and more of the drug. As a result, the price of Ecstasy fell dramatically from £15–£20 in 1987 to as little as £7 in 1996. The price has generally remained steady at around £15 since then.

VERY BRITISH SOLUTIONS

In the UK in the late 1960s, there was growing concern about the proliferation of "hallucinogenic amphetamines" in America, and this prompted a precautionary measure to control specific drugs such as MDA and the more potent TMA. However, in the mid 1970s, police in the Midlands raided an illicit drug laboratory and discovered that the chemist had prepared a hallucinogenic amphetamine that was not

ADVANCED PLEASURE CHEMISTRY

controlled by the law at that time and he was also in possession of the formulae for other drugs of this type. The hallucinogenic amphetamine he had prepared was MDMA – Ecstasy.

In 1977, in order to stay one step ahead of the underground chemists, the Government introduced an amendment to the Misuse of Drugs Act 1971, which was designed to control all amphetamine-like compounds, including MDMA. This amendment put such substances into Class A – the category reserved for those drugs deemed to be the most harmful, where the penalties for possession and dealing are consequently the most severe. A person could face up to seven years in prison plus an unlimited fine for possession, and up to life in prison and an unlimited fine for dealing or trafficking.

MDMA is also in Schedule I of the drug regulations. Schedule I prohibits doctors from prescribing it and, as a Designated Drug, it means that a licence from the Home Office is required before the drug can be used for research purposes of any kind.

Once the iniquities of the rave culture were plastered all over the press, both tabloid and broadsheet, political and social pressure for a law and order response was sure to follow, and it did. Increasing or introducing penalties for drug use has been a key weapon of the state in dealing with youth movements viewed as a threat to society. Initially, police and local authorities relied on legislation such as the 1967 Private Places of Entertaining (Licensing) Act, which requires private as well as public events to be licensed by the local authorities, and the Licensing Act of 1988, which gives the police even greater discretionary powers in the granting of licenses. There was also recourse to various public order legislation, health and safety laws as well as the Misuse of Drugs Act.

Meanwhile, police and partygoers continued to play a cat and mouse game while a whole network of subterfuge was established. The police set up a Pay Party Intelligence Unit based in Kent, to monitor the activities of party or rave organizers. However, it was not the strong-arm tactics of the police that ended the raves, but the introduction of newer and much tougher licensing legislation. Under the new Entertainment (Increased Penalties) Act of 1990, organizers of unlicensed parties could face fines of up to £20,000 and six months in prison. This put most small-scale organizers out of business and most of these moved to the more liberal environment found in European countries such as Germany to continue their trade.

The Criminal Justice Act 1994 (CJA) put the final nail in the coffin of the unlicensed event. For the purpose of the Act, a "rave" is defined as *"a gathering on land in the open air of 100 persons or more... at which amplified music is played during the night... and as such, by reasons of its loudness and duration and the time at which it is played, is likely to cause serious distress to the inhabitants of the locality."* This does not apply to events for which private or public licenses have been granted.

Under the Act, the police can intervene to stop an event from being held, even if only three people have attended, provided a senior police officer has reason to believe that eventually more than a hundred people will gather illegally. The wording of the Act is vague enough to suggest that the complaint of one individual in an otherwise isolated rural location would be enough to stop a party from going ahead.

In May 1998, the Public Entertainments Licences (Drug Misuse) Act came into effect, giving local authorities the power to shut down night-clubs immediately if they find there is evidence of drug use or drug dealing on the premises. This Act allowed the authorities to deal with indoor activities in much the same way as they had with outdoor raves.

ECSTASY FOR THE MASSES

One of the perennial questions that dogs the subject of therapeutic drug use in the field of psychology is the issue of control. How does one control a substance that on the one hand can help therapeutically but on the other also happens to give pleasure to the user?

In Victorian times, the drug scene in the Western hemisphere was very different from that of today. Substantial sections of polite society used drugs like cocaine and marijuana and laudanum (opium and alcohol), provided by a patent-medicine industry run by a handful of men who became exceedingly rich in the process. Even the sovereign, Queen Victoria, was a regular user of laudanum. The drug trade was legitimate at that time. Drugs that are feared and reviled today were standard entries in the medical pharmacopoeias. It is a feature of twentieth-century caution, or paranoia, that those oft-used drugs of yesterday are controlled substances under the law of today.

LEGAL HIGH, LEGAL HAPPINESS

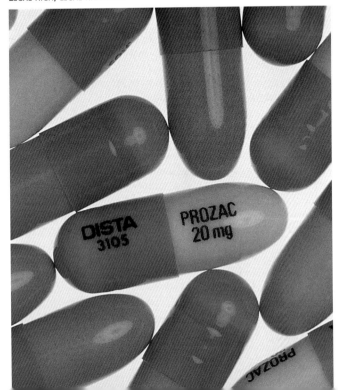

A drug, like any other product or even a person, can be lionized or demonized. All drugs that have gone from the "medicine cabinet to street" started out as being useful to humans and acclaimed for their potential either to alleviate pain, or lift depression, or provide a good night's sleep. During the 1970s and early 1980s, Ecstasy was still in the early hopeful phase of its relationship with society and was being feted all round. Those who used Ecstasy, whether professionally or otherwise, were convinced of its benign qualities and wanted to tell the world about it. Because of its perceived benefits to psychiatry and its empathogenic qualities, Ecstasy received much eulogizing publicity from respectable, mainstream publications in the USA. Exactly the same kind of adulation can be seen in the publicity that has surrounded Prozac. But there has been one major difference – Ecstasy has been banned.

Reputable journals such as *Time* and *Newsweek* have published items praising Ecstasy and its various uses. In 1981, *Wet* magazine ran a feature article entitled, "Everything Looks Wonderful When You're Young and on Drugs", describing the "wondrous effects" of Ecstasy and its widespread distribution. *Life* magazine featured an article in 1985 that referred to the drug's efficacy in helping a woman face up to her cancer less fearfully. The same article included first-hand accounts of people's drug experiences on Ecstasy, stating how it made them more accepting, self-assured, friendly and loving. Yet another magazine, *Harpers Bazaar*, published an item in 1985 revealing that Ecstasy facilitated self-love, self-acceptance, contentment, tranquillity, insight and an ability to *"unravel psychological knots"*. The article went on to describe Ecstasy as being *"the hottest thing in the continuing search for happiness through chemistry"*. All the complimentary publicity only fuelled the American public's desire to get their hands on this wonder drug.

When Prozac, made by the American pharmaceutical company Eli-Lily, came on the market in 1987, it was hailed across the country as a "wonder drug". Since then its sales have soared. In fact, according to analysts at an American investment bank, it is expected that annual sales of Prozac will have hit $4 billion by the year 2000. Ecstasy is a little older than Prozac, but does equally good business. One pill costs approximately £4 to make and sells in the clubs for up to £15. This would suggest that the UK Ecstasy market alone is worth well over £300 million a year.

Both these drugs affect levels of the brain's neurotransmitter serotonin. Neurotransmitters are chemicals that carry messages between nerve cells. They are secreted by one nerve cell and picked up by the receptor proteins on the surface of a neighbouring nerve cell. Once the message has been delivered, the neurotransmitter is destroyed or drawn back into the cell that made it – a process known as re-uptake.

Both Prozac and Ecstasy work by inhibiting or preventing the re-uptake of serotonin. This means that the neurotransmitter molecules hang around in the gap between the nerve cells and the message to the brain is amplified. Ecstasy, in addition to preventing re-uptake, also causes a surge of serotonin to be released into the gap. This means that, not only is the serotonin not removed, but there is more of it there in the first place. Since clinical depression seems to be associated with a deficiency of serotonin, the idea of using serotonin re-uptake inhibitors as anti-depressants has been popular for quite some time.

These are just a few of the parallels between the two drugs and there are several more. But there is an important difference – and one that seems to justify the criminalization of one but not the other. Though Prozac has been charged with inducing violence in occasional cases, it does not cause physical harm to those who use it. Very rarely, Ecstasy, or conditions such as dehydration associated with Ecstasy use, can kill.

The official reason for banning Ecstasy was the fear of neurotoxicity, in as much as it can cause a persistent drop in the natural serotonin levels in the brain. But the DEA, instead of placing the drug in Schedule III, which would have allowed continued medical use, put it in Schedule I, denying it even to the medical community. The real reason for the ban on Ecstasy can be seen more clearly when you take into account the panic on the part of the anti-drugs establishment when Ecstasy went from being taken by small groups in private, to being used by large groups in public.

The history of Prozac shows up the ban on Ecstasy in quite sharp relief. The American Food and Drug Administration accepts Prozac as suitable for the treatment only of depression and obsessive-compulsive disorder and for nothing else. In practice, it is prescribed by thousands of doctors for all sorts of conditions including panic attacks, pre-menstrual tension (PMT) and even premature ejaculation. Increasingly, it is being prescribed to people simply because they want it, just like amphetamines and tranquillizers have been in the past. Those who can't get a sympathetic doctor to write out a prescription are simply turning to the large Prozac black market that already exists.

So, more and more people in the USA are using Prozac simply to make themselves feel better or happier than they normally do – not necessarily to cure any particular medical condition. Considering this, where is the line to be drawn between the therapeutic and non-therapeutic uses of any drug? If there isn't a line already, should there be? If there must be a line, shouldn't it apply equally to all drugs that have the potential for non-therapeutic or hedonistic use?

PHARMACOLOGICAL CALVINISM

The motive for banning drugs that have a non-therapeutic potential is referred to by Dr Peter Kramer, a psychiatrist at Brown University in Providence, Rhode Island, as "pharmacological Calvinism". In his book, *Listening to Prozac*, Dr Brown says that Prozac users more often than not feel *"better than well"*. This is a sentiment that most Ecstasy users would also wholeheartedly agree with. Dr Brown says that: *"Until the advent of Prozac, most ethical questions involving drugs in psychotherapy turned on clinical trade-offs."* But because Prozac has proved to be quite safe and not to have any fatal side-effects, it is more widely prescribed than any other anti-depressant drug in the USA.

The use of drugs for fun rather than therapy has always been widely disapproved of. So, when the pharmacological Calvinists ask whether people taking Prozac to suppress undesirable aspects of their personality, such as excessive shyness, is so far removed or so different from the casual use of Ecstasy, the quite obvious answer would appear to be "no". There is also a feeling, especially within the medical community, that doctors should be the only ones responsible for dispensing drugs. After all, they have the medical training and so know what they're doing. Then why not let these doctors who know what they are doing give out MDMA to their patients, should they choose to, just like the Prozac they already give out by the thousands?

DRUG WARS

In 1996, the UK Government's Chancellor of the Exchequer, Kenneth Clarke, interspersed his 1996 budget speech with mouthfuls of malt whisky. His speech gave the alcohol industry more than one cause for celebration. Not only had the Chancellor given whisky manufacturers some free, prime-time product placement, he had also cut the tax on spirits, thereby boosting the alcohol industry's hopes of increased sales.

In the same year, the UK Government backed a private member's bill in the House of Commons giving local authorities the power to close down dance clubs if they found evidence of drug taking or dealing on the premises. During the passage of this bill through the two Houses of Parliament, numerous references were made specifically to the drug Ecstasy as the main target of this new law. For the alcohol industry, any of the measures that clamped down on the use of Ecstasy were likely to increase sales of alcohol. Drinking alcohol diminishes the effects of Ecstasy, so many people who take the drug tend not to drink alcohol or else cut down consumption quite considerably.

This encroachment by Ecstasy on to the alcohol industry's territory became financially significant in the late 1980s, when the expanding rave culture meant that youth in the UK were increasingly turning away from alcohol and pubs and toward Ecstasy and communal dancing.

A report on the future of leisure in the UK, conducted by the Henley Centre for Forecasting, revealed that between 1987, when the Ecstasy phenomenon began, and 1992, pub attendance in the UK fell by 11 per cent, and a projected 20 per cent decrease was expected by 1997. The Henley Centre also estimated that UK ravers were spending £1.8 billion a year on their clubs and on Ecstasy.

The report concluded: "*This of course poses a significant threat to spending for such sectors as licensed drinks retailers and drink companies. Firstly some young people are turning away from alcohol to stimulants; secondly raves are extremely time consuming and displace much of the time and energy which might have been expended on other leisure activities like pubs or drinking at home.*"

Since the late 1980s there has been a sophisticated war waged between the alcohol industry and rave culture. Large alcohol sales have traditionally always commanded significant lobbying power and this power was put to use in the alcohol industry's battle with the burgeoning rave culture.

In 1989, the leading drinks companies in the UK formed a new public relations alliance. The seven major alcohol manufacturers, including Whitbread, Bass and Seagram, together launched a new PR organization from the headquarters of Guinness plc in London's Portman Square. The Portman Group's stated aim is "*to promote sensible drinking*". However, according to Professor Nick Heather, Director of the Newcastle Centre for Alcohol and Drug Studies, their real agenda is rather different: "*The attempt to distance alcohol as a drug from other kinds of drugs and to give it a good face is the main activity of groups like the Portman Group.*"

A 1994 report entitled *Alcohol and the Public Good*, produced by leading academics and published in conjunction with the World Health Organization (WHO), was adamant and unambiguous in emphasizing the link between alcohol and ill health. This was not the only influential publication that damned alcohol as a dangerous drug. The British Medical Association (BMA) also brought out a report on alcohol in the late 1980s. This report highlighted alcohol's association with 60–70 per cent of homicides, 75 per cent of stabbings and 50 per cent of domestic assaults in the UK. Given these appalling statistics for alcohol, Ecstasy may have seemed like a much safer alternative for ordinary young people. Ecstasy users already knew that they were more likely to be "loved-up" on Ecstasy than violent, as they would be after drinking alcohol.

The emerging implications of any investigations into dangerous drugs, specifically alcohol and Ecstasy, isn't that one is bad and the other good – but that both have their pros and cons and should be treated without any equivocation on the part of government and society. But that is not going to happen. As obvious as it is to most people that alcohol can be seriously bad for you, the amount of money and influence involved in the alcohol business has virtually cemented alcohol's position as a legal and acceptable drug in society.

When the UK's Secretary of State for Health changed the officially recommended limits on alcohol consumption in 1995, he defended his actions like this: *"Alcohol consumption will always be a major public health issue and it is important for the Government to present a balanced view which recognizes the risks but also offers soundly based and credible advice on which people can base their own choices."*

If this approach had been taken when dealing with all other drugs, this statement might have been welcomed as a move toward open debate. Instead, its selective application to alcohol alone is symptomatic of the alcohol industry's deep-seated influence on national politics and culture. On the basis of corporate financial interests rather than concerns for public health and safety, one drug is considered to be socially acceptable while another is not.

AMSTERDAM AHEAD

By the mid 1990s, up to two thirds of clubbers in the city of Amsterdam were using Ecstasy. But the quality of the drug had begun to vary from day to day and from venue to venue. In 1998, Dutch authorities found a large haul of Ecstasy tablets that had been mixed with Atropine, a drug that can cause blindness, permanent heart and breathing problems and even death. The Mayor of Amsterdam was appalled by the quality of the drug available in the city and sent a letter to the city councillors expressing his concerns about the threat to health that impure Ecstasy posed and suggesting a plan he thought might solve the problem.

The Mayor wrote: *"The problem of the polluted market might be met by the controlled sale of Ecstasy, while provision of (health) information could also be enhanced."* His letter went on to say: *"Based on the considerations above, we are not opposed to accepting the motion...we are willing to study the conditions under which controlled sale of Ecstasy is possible."*

In December 1998, the Mayor proposed to councillors that the City should consider organizing supervised sales of Ecstasy, although he admitted that this would be difficult to arrange under current Dutch law. The law in the Netherlands tolerates the sale and use of "soft" drugs such as cannabis, while retaining quite tough penalties for anyone dealing in "hard" drugs. At present, Ecstasy falls into the hard-drugs category.

Historically, the Dutch have had one of the most forward thinking and open-minded attitudes to drug use in Europe. Their methods have been rooted in the harm-reduction view of drug law enforcement and drug users are not demonized or criminalized as they are in other parts of the world. This approach by the Dutch has not always earned them friends in other governments, but young people who get into trouble with drugs in the Netherlands are more likely to turn to the authorities for help than they are in other countries, as they are more likely to get a helping hand and less likely to face official opprobrium.

The Amsterdam city authorities decided to spend time initiating further research into the subject and have said that they will try to make a decision one way or the other by the year 2000. Something that might help them to reach that decision is a recent drug law development elsewhere in Europe – in Switzerland.

SWITZERLAND AND ECSTASY

The view that most law enforcers in Europe take toward Ecstasy has been the product of panic, to say the least. During the 1990s, Ecstasy slipped into the role of the new "bogeyman" in the on-going "war against drugs" and there has been almost no real scientific research or rational debate over the drug. By contrast, in 1999, Switzerland's Supreme Court ruled that dealing in Ecstasy is not a serious offence. Ecstasy remains illegal, but is now regarded by the law as a soft drug rather than a hard one, as the authorities consider that it cannot be said to pose a serious risk to physical and mental health and does not generally lead to criminal behaviour. The Swiss legal establishment took the view that the people who use Ecstasy are generally "socially integrated people".

This decision was made at a Swiss Federal Tribunal that overturned a ruling by a local Berne court that had sentenced a man to over a year in prison for selling one thousand Ecstasy pills. The Tribunal found that, according to the research that had been put before it, Ecstasy was not as chemically toxic or socially dangerous as had previously been assumed. It was even thought that Ecstasy might have some positive properties after all. Studies of the kind that so influenced the Swiss court are very rare at the moment because very few governments allow or license legitimate, funded Ecstasy research programmes.

The leniency of the Tribunal's ruling is proof of an open-minded attitude toward Ecstasy which is also evident in the Swiss policy toward research into the drug. Between 1988 and 1993, psychotherapists in private practice were allowed to administer Ecstasy to their patients in a controlled environment as an aid to therapy. MDMA research is also currently underway at the Psychiatric University Hospital, in Zurich. Researchers there have been given permission by the government to conduct studies in which MDMA is administered to regular users and to "MDMA-naïve" volunteers. The results will be used to build up a body of medical evidence as to the various therapeutic properties of MDMA.

REPUTATIONS

It would be fair to say that a new form of black music appears in the USA every ten years or so, only to be tamed, toned down and co-opted into the mainstream. The next generation of black musicians will then come along, having fashioned yet another innovative new style, to re-establish the identity of black music and its origins in the homes and communities. It is easy to see in hindsight how, in succession, blues, soul and funk were appropriated and absorbed into the white mainstream until, by the 1970s, it was time for something completely different.

The 1970s were the hey-day of disco. This new music created an energetic dance scene founded on the passion of expert musicians who dazzled when they were playing their drums, bass, guitar and strings. But things were soon to change. With the release of the movie *Saturday Night Fever* in 1978, disco seemed to boom across the country. But what the film had also done was take an underground black phenomenon and put it on the mass market. In the process, an interesting and vibrant music scene was caricatured, made to shed its black context, sanitized of its gay element, totally whitewashed and ironed out for popular, mainstream acceptance and consumption. The film turned disco into a multi-million dollar business but it also turned it into what seemed like a cheap, trashy, transient fad. Soon, disco was considered frivolous, throwaway and commercial – "Disco Sucks" became the new refrain of the hip insiders.

In the meantime, a series of records were beginning to appear that used computer technology to revolutionize the existing disco sound. Much of this new sound was linked to the European electronic traditions that the USA was slowly getting into, the impact of the German band Kraftwerk arguably being the strongest. Many pioneering New York DJs such as Afrika Bambaataa can take credit for the seismic shift in music that was soon to overwhelm the USA.

He created a unique mix of the Jamaican tradition of chatting on the mike, intertwined with electronic music inspired by Kraftwerk.

Bambaataa paid this tribute: *"I don't think they* [Kraftwerk] *even knew how big they were among the black masses... when they came out with Trans Europe Express. I thought that was one of the best and weirdest records I ever heard in my life... It was funky."*

LEVAN'S GARAGE

Evolving technology meant that music now seemed to be infused with all sorts of new creative possibilities. No longer was music made by musical instruments alone. The studios and their recording equipment became the new musical instruments. The most important exponent of this new movement was Larry Levan, a Brooklyn-born DJ who appeared every weekend at a New York club called the Paradise Garage. Levan, a dance music fanatic, had custom-designed the club's music system, soon considered one of the best in the world. Clubbers in the Big Apple vied with one another to get into the club and dance the night away.

Larry Levan, born Lawrence Philpot in 1954, started his DJ-ing career in the early 1970s. He gained a reputation for being someone who could put clubbers into a trance with the music he played and the way he played it. Regular visitors to the club remember being almost "transported into another world on a shared journey". Though the clubbers of the day pay tribute to Levan for giving them a sense of release through the music he played, many forget to mention that chemicals also played an important part in the way they were feeling. MDA, Ecstasy's parent drug, known on the streets, as the "love drug", and speed were both popular in clubs at that time. Ecstasy was beginning to make an appearance at the club, too. It had made the move from Texas and California and was popping up in all sorts of venues around the country. Dancers who were trying it for the first time were amazed at what it did for them.

Music's potential to put people into a trance was not a new 1970s phenomenon. In fact, it can be traced all the way back to the twelfth century Sufi poet Jalal'uddin Rumi, who would enter ecstatic trances while singing praises to Allah and whirling round and round. Of course, this dancing wasn't drug-induced, but inspired by the ecstasies of worship, and by dancing and rejoicing in the praise and love of Allah. Rumi's followers practise the tradition to this day in the Turkish town of Konya, where they have become world famous as the "whirling dervishes". The culture of Candomble in South America also involves adepts falling into a trance and swaying frenetically to the rhythm of the drums as if under a spell.

Levan's musical taste was very eclectic. He played almost anything that captured the devotional, life-affirming feel that he was after – whether it was disco, soul, rock, gospel, reggae or pop. Mel Cheren, one of the backers of the Paradise Garage club, described his abilities: *"He would experiment with records that other people wouldn't go near. He really was an engineering genius as far as sound was concerned – they even have speakers named after him. He was brilliant."*

Levan's approach to his music was much like a scientist's attitude to his laboratory experiments. Levan knew that people in his club were using drugs and it was his job to maximize their effects. He mixed sounds as if he was knowingly playing with the chemistry of each person's mind and body. A fellow New York DJ put it succinctly: *"Larry invented new levels of bass and treble that worked on various parts of your body."* By now, the partying stakes in New York were much higher. Levan could gauge the pulse of the party people and he knew that the drugs on the street were also an integral influence on the kind of music he played, *"The way people party now, the drugs that are in the street, everything has got to be wild and crazy and electronic,"* he said.

At the Garage, people were taking all sorts of drugs to lift their spirits, including LSD, mescaline, cocaine, speed and, of course, Ecstasy. The club buzzed with different kinds of energy – sexual, spiritual, musical and chemical. On the floor could be found black and Puerto Rican gay men swinging their bodies with wild abandon, and frenzied dancers stripped down to their shorts and sweating it out. The word was out about the Ecstasy effect and soon anyone who was anyone on the club scene was seeking out Ecstasy specifically. The energy of disco music was demanding a corresponding level of dance energy and so the drug's capacity to heighten mood and increase energy in partygoers was just what was needed.

Levan appeared at the Garage from 1976 until it closed down in 1987. After it closed, Levan's notorious capacity for drugs began to reach dangerous levels. New York clubland legend has it that he spent all his money on chemicals and went on a self-destructive binge. He missed gigs he was booked to attend, procrastinated over studio work and, inevitably, his health steadily declined. This pioneer of the new club generation died of heart failure in 1992, aged only 38.

THE BIRTH OF HOUSE

While Larry Levan was spinning discs in New York he was helping to create a club model that was to travel far and wide. The atmosphere inside his club, almost devotional in its intensity, was highly sought after. The rapture and excitement found in early dance clubs in the USA was born out of necessity. Many black people were excluded from the economic and social benefits of the American dream, homosexuals were excluded from the mainstream moral world of American society and black gay men couldn't even express their

FRANKIE KNUCKLES – TRANSPORTING CLUBBERS TO ANOTHER PLANE

identity within their own communities. This pent-up frustration found its release in the dance clubs, the only place where they could be themselves without any worries. The clubs allowed gay men a place to be free and Ecstasy enabled them to release all the stress that had been building up inside them. The energy explosion in the clubs was huge and so was the sense of bonding – no doubt helped along by the copious amount of drugs that were being consumed.

In 1977, Frankie Knuckles, a colleague of Larry Levan's, moved west to Chicago, Illinois, having learnt all he could from the best in the business. He had been asked to play at a club called the Warehouse. He remembers the club as being *"predominantly black and predominantly gay. Very soulful, very spiritual. For most of the people that went there, it was church for them. It only happened one day a week: Saturday night into Sunday morning into Sunday afternoon. In the early days, the parties were very intense."*

At first, Knuckles was playing the classic gay disco anthems for his new audience. But soon he began to mess around with the sound itself: taking records apart and re-editing them, extending certain bits, losing other bits and rearranging the sound to give the dancers in the club an extra kick. He had seen it done before in New York and knew that it worked – but this was astonishingly new to Chicago and soon everyone was clamouring to get into the club.

Knuckles and his new Warehouse sound were complemented perfectly by the dance music show on the local radio station WBMX. The "Hot Mix 5" crew were a group of young turntable magicians who excelled at mixing rapid-fire musical and sound collages. These five DJs carried the new sounds and atmosphere of the clubs straight on to the airwaves and into society.

At about the same time, a rival club in Chicago called the Music Box had found itself a mad new musical scientist called Ron Hardy. Hardy played records with a raw energy that "made the moment". People who came to his club, came to live for the moment of his music. He seemed to have amazing control over the dance-floor and to be able to elicit pure, clear energy out of the music he played, a sound that seemed to be charged with adrenaline. Inspirational music producer Marshall Jefferson, a regular at the Music Box, said: *"Ron Hardy was the greatest DJ who ever lived."* The kids at the Warehouse christened Frankie Knuckles' luscious soulful sounds "House music". But across town at the Music Box, kids were using the same name to describe Hardy's rougher, more battering mixes.

The Music Box was a no-alcohol venue that played music for dance lovers. Because there was no alcohol, there was an underlying symbiotic relationship between drugs and music that helped to change ordinary sound into magic and disco into House. Most dancers at the club were using some drug or other. But the drug that pretty much took over the scene was Ecstasy. With its ability to make the music almost curl around your spine and force you to dance against your will, Ecstasy was much sought after by the serious hedonists.

The phenomenon coming out of all these different clubs was inspiring a host of young people to make new music. This music was mainly released on crackling 12-inch records on Chicago's two main independent record labels, Trax and DJ International. Many have since tried to describe and define the exact sound of House music. But these fast, raw, hard, exciting new sounds seemed as far removed as possible from anything that had gone before. Farley "Jackmaster" Funk, one of the five WBMX radio station DJs says it's very simple: *"House music wasn't nothing but disco, and proof of that is to listen to all the early House records. All we did was steal people's music... House music ain't nothing but a harder kick drum than disco, that's it."* New technology had thrown open the creative process to all musicians and the Ecstasy had removed all inhibitions, even musical ones.

TECHNO HEAVEN

Across the Illinois state border in Detroit, Michigan, another hub of musical activity was developing and having a powerful effect on the dance scene. Until then, Detroit had mainly been famous as the legendary home of soul music. But Detroit DJs were playing with sounds and using technology to voyage into new musical territory.

Juan Atkins and Richard Davis, a Vietnam veteran, formed an electronic music group called Cybotron. They were heavily influenced by the European sound, but had their roots in black American funk traditions. Atkins was a musical preacher who introduced a couple of his young friends, Derrick May and Kevin Saunderson, to electronic music such as the sounds of Kraftwerk, Human League and Gary Numan. As committed clubbers, they in turn introduced him to what was being played currently in clubs across America – the Chicago House sound.

After Cybotron split up, all three friends started solo projects. These three black men, through their music, escaped from Detroit into a different state, much as many had done before. As Paul Gilroy, the black cultural theorist puts it in his seminal book *Ain't No Black in the Union Jack*, *"The dream of life beyond the reach of racism acquired an other-worldly, utopian quality and then manifested itself in a flash, high-tech form deliberately remote from the realities of the ghetto lifeworld. If the repressive and destructive forces unleashed by a 'maggot-brained' and infanticidal America were rapidly acquiring a global character, the answer to them was presented as flight... into space."*

As well as being the home of soul, Detroit was also the "Motor City". During the late 1950s and 1960s, the American car market was huge and Detroit was the Mecca of all things motor-driven. Assembly-line car production had brought a new wealth and standard of living to the city. But, with every boom there comes a bust, and the American motor industry was no exception. Only a couple of decades earlier, Detroit had spawned the feel-good, up-time soul music of Motown, but now the auto bosses were closing factories down and laying many workers off.

Atkins, May and Saunderson used any equipment they could lay their hands on to create a "drubby" sound with huge drums. This music was also mournful – almost as mournful as the sound of factory machines being shut down. People in Detroit took to this music. It made them dance and forget. This was the sound of what it felt like to be young and black in post-industrial America. They called it "Techno". Techno seemed very different from the other Ecstasy-soaked sounds popular at the time, but it was only a matter of time and the sheer, relentless beat of Techno found a perfect partner in Ecstasy.

GROUND-BREAKING SOUNDS

Out of the clubs in New York, Chicago and Detroit had come sounds that would change the world of popular music. Garage, House and Techno were three interlinked threads with the same premise of using technology to heighten and increase pleasure and perception and also to help transport young clubbers away from their depressed everyday existences. All these new sounds playing in the clubs across America had one magical collaborator – Ecstasy. The drug had started out merely as an accompaniment to the sounds, but by the time the sounds reached the mainstream, so had Ecstasy. The drug was now virtually driving the rhythm on.

PIONEERING BRITONS

It is widely believed that Ecstasy first came to the UK from Ibiza around the mid 1980s. This is part of the Ecstasy story – but there is another part that began much earlier. In the early 1980s, two Britons, Marc Almond and Dave Ball, went to New York to record their first album as Soft Cell. Soft Cell was one of a whole host of synthesizer bands around at that time. Almond remembers listening to Kraftwerk when he was growing up in Leeds and believed that synthesizers would revolutionize the music scene. Soft Cell already had one hit single in Britain, "Tainted Love", a cover version of an old Northern Soul classic, which had become the best selling single of 1981.

When these two party animals got to New York, they were turned on by something they had never tried before – Ecstasy. According to Almond, their debut album *Non Stop Erotic Cabaret* – was the first British Ecstasy record: "*It became a whole album that was done all around Ecstasy and done on Ecstasy – when we listened to the mixes of the album we took Ecstasy to listen to them. It sounded absolutely fantastic.*"

The album was followed up by a collection of remixes – *Non Stop Ecstatic Dancing*. The video of one track, "Memorabilia", showed Almond and

MARC ALMOND

Ball in a New York cityscape with their local drug dealer Cindy delivering these lines: *"We can take a pill and shut our eyes and let our love materialize. I don't mean love on a chocolate box, I mean love that really rocks, because they call me the baby; the good time lady; just look at me and it's easy to see why they call me Cindy Ecstasy."* Few people in London had heard of Ecstasy in the early 1980s, so when the song was released in Britain, most people had no idea what they were talking about and they got away with the reference to the drug. Ecstasy was a key influence in the way Soft Cell developed its sound. It would be fair to say that their first three albums were made around the drug and the whole Ecstasy "feeling".

A few years later, Boy George (O'Dowd), who was then at the height of his success with the band Culture Club, would have a very similar experience with Ecstasy. In his candid autobiography, *Take It Like a Man*, George O'Dowd describes how taking Ecstasy for the first time seemed like the perfect treatment for the increasingly isolated life he was having to lead as a pop star: *"After half an hour, the drug hit me like a sensuous tidal wave. I turned into a tactile temptress and wanted to stroke the whole world. It gave me untold confidence... The next morning I woke feeling liberated, like I'd opened Pandora's pillbox and found the meaning of life. I wanted to buy a whole bag of 'E'."*

Boy George was famously anti-drugs, until he got caught up in a drugs spiral after moving to New York. Following a successful battle against addiction, George cleaned up his act and plugged into the new club culture buzzing around him. For a long while, he stayed away from clubs and other night-spots for fear of being tempted to take drugs again. Now, he is one of the few pop acts who has managed to cross from the stage to the club floor where he has become a much loved and eagerly sought after club DJ.

Once people returning to the UK from New York started to spread the word about Ecstasy, it seemed that everyone wanted to try it. The first trickle of supplies were sent over from New York in envelopes or brought back by adventurous travellers. The few anointed and chosen people in London would wait for the return of the couriers and the much sought-after fancy stuff they were carrying. During the period between 1982 and 1986, the people who were using Ecstasy in the UK were the Soho elite – club runners, club celebrities, music writers, models and international pop stars. In those early days in London, Ecstasy was used as a private party drug and not as a dance club drug as it was in the USA. These parties would be little gatherings of the chosen, at a private home, where people would take Ecstasy and loll on the settees, talking and messing around. The mood was playful, and not serious or spiritual.

THE TRUTH SEEKERS

At the same time that the beautiful people were enjoying their Ecstasy experience – another group of Londoners, across the city in Hampstead, were also being initiated into the Ecstasy experience. These initiates were followers of the therapeutic, rather than the hedonistic school of Ecstasy. In 1985, *Face* magazine published the first article on Ecstasy in the UK. Journalist Peter Nasmyth had befriended the radical Scottish psychiatrist R.D. Laing, who believed that MDMA showed great promise as an aid to psychotherapy.

Laing opened the way for Nasmyth to take an intimate gaze into this world of middle-class intellectuals. *"Most of the people I interviewed were involved in some kind of group or therapy or organization and they were all proselytizing it. Again they were very often sixties or seventies people who were looking for the new sacrament and were very keen to believe that Ecstasy was it."* Nasmyth came across some resistance when he was writing his article – many in the group did not want any publicity for Ecstasy. They wanted to keep it for themselves and to hide it away from the attention of the world at large.

In the same year the *Face* article was published, the first seizures of Ecstasy were made in the UK. A couple of London clubs were now starting to hold Ecstasy parties, even though the drug was still in short supply. At venues such as Taboo and the Hug Club, clubbers were really enjoying themselves on Ecstasy. At the Hug Club they would queue up to get their Ecstasy tabs in an orderly manner, as they were quite precious. The drug was flown in specially from New York – clubbers were allowed one tab each and no more. But in those early days of good quality gear and low resistance – one Ecstasy tab was more than enough to have a very good time indeed. This London Ecstasy scene was very much a closed shop – full of a smug elite who didn't want to share their fun and for a while it seemed as if Ecstasy was going to die a death somewhere in a Soho club – unless something out of the ordinary came along to free it up.

IBIZA SUNSHINE

The seemingly unstoppable rise of Ecstasy in the UK can now easily be traced back to the west Mediterranean holiday island of Ibiza and the year 1987. Until the 1960s, Ibiza had been an obscure rural community in the Balearic Isles, with a population of about 37,000 people. By the middle of the 1960s, though, things had started to change. Spain, under General Franco, was encouraging the tourist trade to Ibiza and soon the once desolate and beautiful island had become a hive of greasy cafes, souvenir shops, pubs and hotels and its towns were beginning to fill with British and German holidaymakers. Ibiza also attracted beatniks, hippies and backpackers who came to the island for its sun and the peaceful atmosphere. Soon the hippies had set up their own communes and their own supply lines for drugs. By the mid 1960s, Ibiza had become an essential, almost mandatory stop on the hippie trail.

Many Spanish people also flocked to Ibiza as they saw it as a haven free from the restrictions of Fascist life under General Franco. Religious cults, including the acolytes of Bhagwan Rajneesh, also established bases on the island. Ibiza began to take on a personality tinged with a bit of everything – hippie dreams, gay flamboyance, jet-set glamour and the inevitable banality of tourist growth. As one local DJ puts it: *"The hippie influence is really basic because the spirit really comes from them – that freedom and wild kind of life. That's the heritage and the real spirit of Ibiza – free parties, open air, the moon and the stars, good music, dancing... The hippie thing is finished, but they've been used in a way to give an image of Ibiza to the rest of Europe – the free island, the island of love."*

As unemployment grew in the UK, a new breed of tourist reached the island. These were young people for whom slave-wage jobs or dole subsistence just wasn't the answer. They were happier to get out of the UK and catch some fun and sun. They would travel around the Mediterranean – Tenerife in the winter, Ibiza in the summer. They survived by doing odd jobs in bars, clubs or restaurants or by petty theft or selling hashish. Anything was better than staying in miserable, grey Britain.

There were two main nightclubs on the island at that time. Pasha opened in 1973, playing reggae and rock to the hippies. Amnesia was just a run-down farm with no electricity. Hippies and Bhagwan Rajneesh disciples would get together and dance around bonfires, while others played music or just sat around and smoked dope. By the time the hippie movement was over, Ibiza's clubs had gone through the most amazing metamorphosis. These weren't discos as anyone else knew them – they had outdoor dance floors under the moon and stars, huge fountains, palm trees and flamboyant décor that was constantly changing. All sorts of people began to flood into the clubs – flash millionaires, pop stars, showy gays of all ages and nationalities. These weren't ordinary clubs anymore; they had become dream playgrounds.

Ecstasy started to enter Ibiza in the early 1980s, following the same routes that the various travellers had taken. Until then, the main drugs on the island were LSD, dope and cocaine. But when the first House music imports started to flood in – so did Ecstasy. In 1987, British DJ Trevor Fung and his cousin Ian St Paul opened a bar in San Antonio, the island's main town. The Project, as it was called, became a focal point for British holidaymakers, a hub for many of the key people who would go on to form the heart of the "Acid House" scene in Britain.

In the different island nightclubs such as Pasha, Amnesia and Ku, a small group of British holidaymakers, from the north and the south, first experienced the heady mix of Ecstasy and electronic dance music. The small groups of predominantly young working-class Britons who had stood on the sidelines of society were now right in the thick of things. They would meet in bars in town and then head out to the clubs, where they would take their Ecstasy and raise the roof until the sun came up. They would then spend the day winding down and relaxing, only to wind themselves back up again for the next night of carousing with another tab of Ecstasy. They were on holiday and they were having fun. The real world was a million miles away. The fantastic sense of unreality that they were creating was carried along by Ecstasy. It helped them bond with each other like they had never bonded before.

IBIZA – FALLING IN LOVE WITH ECSTASY

ECSTASY'S "FIRST FAMILY"

Fung and St Paul invited their friend Paul Oakenfold, a former chef turned DJ, to Ibiza for a holiday. Oakenfold brought along two of his friends, DJ Johnny Walker and club promoter Nicky Holloway, and Holloway invited another of his DJ friends along, Danny Rampling. What happened next, as they say, is history. The earlier footloose and fancy-free clubbers had already set the scene for this enchanted group. Ecstasy was a big mind-opener for them all. In their own words, they came back to the UK *"like salesmen for the stuff..."*

Soon, the Ibiza season was over. Influenced by their summertime experiences, these upwardly-mobile clubbers and DJs tried to recreate their summer holiday atmosphere in London clubs. Initially, they would go to the handful of clubs, such as Delirium, that were playing Acid House music, and to gay club nights like Pyramid. But none of these venues had the atmosphere the group was looking for. So they decided to use their Club Ibiza experiences to replicate the island sounds of summer and fire up the waning London club scene themselves. St Paul and Oakenfold started opening the Project after hours, from 2–6am. The Ibiza coterie would come in through the back door and the fun would begin. This didn't last very long – they were raided – but they had sowed the seeds. E culture was born in the UK.

"SHOOMING"

Of that small group, one person in particular was very deeply influenced by Ecstasy and its club possibilities – Danny Rampling. Toward the end of 1987, he and his wife, Jenni, threw a party. The title of the event, "Shoom", was supposed to be a description of how you felt when the first rush of Ecstasy kicked in. It was a good night, but not quite as good as the gang remembered it being in Ibiza. So, a few weeks later, they booked the annexe to the huge gay club Heaven and held a party night called "Future". This time it was much more successful.

The period from late 1987 to the middle of 1988 was a journey of discovery for the group. They had a great new music that you couldn't hear in the mainstream, a great new vibe that couldn't be found elsewhere and a new collective consciousness that was definitely unique. They felt as if they were shedding their old prejudices and habits and leaving their past lives behind them. Ecstasy had opened up some kind of door and all manner of bizarre phenomena were streaming in.

The "Shoom" and "Future" experience was growing – people wanted to bring friends, and friends wanted to bring yet more friends and soon there wasn't enough room for everybody. Having started out as the

OAKENFOLD – "SHOOM"-ING TO FAME AND FORTUNE

secret fixation of hip insiders from London, House music was soon sliding down-market and causing the most splendid upheaval of London and suburban night-life. Where Ecstasy wasn't yet available, LSD was swallowed, sometimes in combination with speed.

The clubs, with their restrictive spaces and opening hours, proved too small to contain the phenomenon and demand grew for bigger parties. St Paul and Oakenfold saw an opportunity and, in April 1988, booked the entire Heaven club – with the capacity to hold fifteen hundred people – for one night. Everybody told them they were fools, but they stuck with it. Fewer than a hundred people turned up on that first night. They continued with the bookings and by the third week they were deep in debt and thinking of calling it all off. They gave themselves one more week before deciding. Whether it was their good karma or just effective word of mouth, the fourth week saw queues stretching all the way from the club to Charing Cross Station! Everyone wanted in on the fun. Ironically, they had dubbed the club night "Spectrum: Theatre of Madness".

The distinctive, cosy warmth and glow of the early days had dissipated and the crowds grew and grew. As Ecstasy was so crucial to this scene, the demand for the drug was on the up. Ecstasy distribution had stepped up a couple of gears and a lot more people were being introduced to this magical new substance. People became so involved in the vibe that many of them started dealing, whether it was buying a few for their friends or buying pills in bulk and selling them on.

BIRTH OF THE "RAVE NATION"

As this new Ecstasy-filled tidal wave washed over the club scene, Nicky Holloway opened "The Trip" at the famous Astoria club. It was at this point that the Acid House scene officially went public – and commercial. Now it was for the masses. The old elite damned Holloway as a philistine who had jumped on the bandwagon and was cashing in on the trend. But "The Trip" lived up to its name. When the club closed at 3am, people would spill out on to Charing Cross Road and have a spontaneous street party – still dancing. "The Trip" opened up Acid House to the inner-city working classes and boxed it up for the media and music industry, bringing in a multi-racial crowd that had certainly not been seen during the early days at "Shoom" or "Future", where the partygoers had been exclusively white.

Ibiza, Rampling, "Shoom", St Paul, Oakenfold, "Spectrum", Holloway, "The Trip" – so runs the formal history of Acid House and Ecstasy in the UK. But like every story told, there is always a part that is, more often than not, left untold. There was, from the very beginning, another strand within London House culture that was composed of people who had never been to Ibiza, but had connections with the black dance collectives of north London and roots in the warehouse party phenomenon from the 1980s.

These people showcased the latest music from Chicago, Detroit and New York and were creating a new audience for House music that wasn't run by the traditional white music hierarchy. They had felt excluded by "Shoom's" predominantly white, south-London attendance and so they created their own Ecstasy wonderlands. There was no opulent décor in their venues – just dry ice and strobe lights. The important thing was dancing – nothing else mattered. House music and culture and Ecstasy were now beginning to demonstrate how inclusive they were and how adaptable they could be. It changed shape and form depending on the venue, the people, the drugs and the environment.

This state of grace would not continue for much longer. In August 1988, *The Sun* newspaper published a major investigation into the new drug scene at the night-club Heaven (owned by Richard Branson), complete with a picture of a blotter of acid. *"Scandal of the £5 drug trip to Heaven"* shouted the headline and it continued in the same vein, *"LSD – a favourite with 1970s dropouts – is now popular with yuppies."* Without doing any real research, the paper took the term "Acid

House" literally, assuming that "Acid" meant LSD. Today, their ignorance may seem ridiculous. But when it comes to a drugs story, it can often seem that sensationalism and shock value are much more important than the facts.

At around the same time as they were exhorting Richard Branson to shut his night-club, *The Sun* also printed an "Acid House fashion guide" and began marketing its own Smiley T-shirts. *"It's groovy and cool. Only £5.50 man."* The next week, the paper was running a series of articles on the *"evil of Ecstasy"*. The paper's medical columnist Vernon Coleman warned:

"You will hallucinate... Hallucinations can last up to 12 hours... There's a good chance you'll end up in a mental hospital for life... If you're young enough, there's a good chance you'll be sexually assaulted while under the influence and you may not even know until a few days or weeks later."

Hysteria took hold immediately. The Top Shop chain of stores banned Smiley shirts and the BBC's "Top of the Pops" chart show declared a freeze on all records containing the word "acid".

After *The Sun* published its article, Paul Oakenfold took a break, changed the name of the club night and opened up again a month later. Renamed as the Land of Oz, the club night ran for years.

PARTNERS IN PLEASURE

Tony Colston-Hayter was the son of a solicitor and a university lecturer, whose parents had divorced when he was still very young. Even as a young boy he had shown a great gift for making money. While still at school in Buckinghamshire, he set up three companies, Colston Automatics, Colston Leisure and Colston Marketing.

Dave Roberts came from the other side of the tracks. He was a young, black, working-class, north-London lad, whose elder brothers were well known among the "faces" at Arsenal Football Club's Highbury ground. Roberts had a charming and forceful personality that drove him into the property business at an early age.

The two men's paths crossed for the first time in 1987, when Colston-Hayter decided to go into the property business and ran into Roberts. They clicked immediately. For two young men who had grown up in Thatcher's Britain, the economic potential of the yuppie 1980s was a temptation they gave in to happily. Both of them would work hard cooking up all sorts of big plans to make the money they wanted.

But work wasn't the whole story – they played hard too. As two larger-than-life characters on the club scene, it was inevitable that Roberts and Colston-Hayter would end up at "Shoom" in the early days. Their first weekend was a revelation to both of them. But as

"Shoom's" door policy slowly become more restrictive and the Ibiza crowd began to close ranks, Roberts and Colston-Hayter found they weren't considered a part of this special gang. The "Shoom" crowd wanted to keep their playground to themselves and didn't want anyone else crashing the party.

Meanwhile, "The Trip" had opened up at the Astoria and Nicky Holloway didn't have a special door policy there. His whole drive had been to open the House scene to the widest possible group and so make the most money. This suited Roberts and his friends. They would turn up at the club and, along with everybody else, go wild dancing. There was something special about being in a large crowd where everybody was on the same "vibe" and so "The Trip" was a smash hit. Not much alcohol was being drunk, everybody felt "loved up" on Ecstasy.

Being a connoisseur of the good life, Colston-Hayter had dabbled a bit in club promotion himself, running a few small gigs. But he had never felt anything like the party vibe he experienced during 1987 and 1988. Nothing like Ecstasy had happened to the club scene before and he wasn't going to let the opportunity pass. He knew almost instantly that this scene was going to be big. And he planned big – he wanted to have parties catering for thousands and not just hundreds. He wanted all classes, all races, all colours, shapes and sizes dancing and having a good time together.

Colston-Hayter's first "Apocalypse Now" events at Wembley Studios in August 1988 pulled in a very diverse range of club people. The multitude cut across all lines of race and class, and there was a mellow, happy feel, right through the crowd, courtesy of Ecstasy.

Enthused by his success, Colston-Hayter invited ITN's *News at Ten* to come and see what happens at one of his gigs. Unfortunately, he timed it badly. By the middle of 1988, the first wave of tabloid hysteria about Ecstasy culture was breaking. Inevitably, the press wasn't interested in reflecting the rise of a particular music culture, they stayed focused on the drugs. The ITN news item did Colston-Hayter no favours, but drew the attention of the police to his activities. A little police interest wasn't going to deter this entrepreneur, however.

He renamed his organization "Sunrise" and set out to continue his work. The police raided the very first Sunrise party he put on, and he lost all the money he had made. But even though his costs seemed to be outstripping his profits, this was a minor setback for a compulsive chancer. If the law was going to dog his footsteps in London – he was going to party elsewhere. He sold a thousand tickets for a "Sunrise Mystery Trip" and booked coaches to take clubbers from London to Iver Heath, near his home in Buckinghamshire, where he had taken over an equestrian centre for the day. The "Mystery Trip" was a resounding success for all involved. Ecstasy had cast its spell and Colston-Hayter had been well and truly bitten by the party bug.

Buoyed up by this success, he chose a massive venue for his next party – the "Sunrise Guy Fawkes Edition" – a huge derelict gasworks in south London. This was going to be a spectacular production – 3000 tickets had been sold. But as the event got under way, riot police flooded the area, shutting down the music and blocking the approach road. The people were not to be deterred so easily, however, and they climbed over fences and scrambled over dual carriageways in a running battle with the law. The police were forced to give up and withdraw.

This kind of conflict was shocking to the old Ibiza crowd – they felt that the early spirit had been soured. What was more, the promoters had been filmed during the confrontation and the tabloid press had found their demon. Tony Colston-Hayter was now dubbed the "Acid-House King". Nevertheless, he continued with his plans to hold Christmas and New Year's parties in Hackney. It was here that he came up against a more explosive force than the police. A group of "faces" from the West Ham football terraces wanted a "slice of the action" from the parties that were being held on "their" territory. They too understood the limitless opportunities that Ecstasy had recently helped open up. Colston-Hayter now needed help and he turned to his friend Dave Roberts – who had stayed out of the business until then. Roberts was brought in to "stabilize" the football thugs and any others who might try to take advantage.

TECHNOLOGY TO THE RESCUE

Colston-Hayter went back to the country to escape all the unwanted attention. He spent a lot of time trying to think of a way to outsmart the authorities and still have a good time. He needed to come up with an inventive and hitherto unheard of tactic. He finally hit upon the answer by hiring BT's Voice Bank system. This system provides numerous telephone lines into a single answering machine and allows the user to change the message remotely from a mobile phone. With a secret ticketing arrangement that hooked up hundreds of lines to a computer system, Colston-Hayter could direct clubbers to an area, wait until numbers had reached a critical mass, and then release the address for the party over the Voice Bank system and fill the site before the police knew what was going on.

As many as a thousand cars and scores of vans full of young people would gather at a pre-arranged meeting point – typically somewhere on the M25. Then, once a large enough crowd had gathered, he would send out the exact location of the party venue and there would be a mad rush to get there before the police did. These gatherings were now becoming unstoppable. The parties steadily got bigger and bigger, soon attracting ten thousand people or more as a matter of course. Needless to say, they also continued to get the attention of a disapproving tabloid press.

Things carried on like this until the summer of 1989. And a hot summer it was too – the hottest in over a decade. There is something about a hot summer in the UK that always seems to un-stiffen the British upper lip and raise the national mood, encouraging the country to go out and have a good time. This was an old tradition, but a lot of things had changed. Ecstasy was now working its magic on all sorts of new people. Huge numbers of people were being converted to a new way of partying as each new group tried Ecstasy and liked it. The parties were no longer called parties; they had become "raves", yet another term taken from the black soul scene.

Sunrise's "Midsummer Night's Dream Party" at White Waltham airfield in Berkshire put the rave phenomenon on the map – in case anyone had missed it before. This was a very big party, and a lot of work had gone into making it just right for those that had bought the tickets. But unknown to the promoters, in among the eleven thousand or more ravers was a group of tabloid reporters. *The Sun* set the tone on Monday morning with a grisly account of very young girls, spaced out on drugs, rubbing shoulders with dangerous dealers and drug-crazed young men jumping around to a lot of noise, while the police looked on helplessly.

The *Daily Mail* added its weight with a grave editorial warning of "A New Threat to British Youth". What both newspapers had omitted to mention was that there had been no drugs arrests at the party. When asked about drugs at his gigs, Colston-Hayter denied all knowledge. *"I don't take drugs, I don't sell them, and we don't have them at our parties."*

Many did not believe him. Disturbed by all this negative law and order publicity, Douglas Hurd, the Home Secretary at the time, ordered an immediate enquiry into unlicensed parties in Britain.

GATHERING STORMS

The rave phenomenon was getting a fair amount of critical press, but nothing as yet that would stop the party, until one fateful night in August 1989. Colston Hayter and Roberts were planning the "Sunrise/Back to the Future Dance Music Festival". They had found a farm they could use as the venue for the event and had just concluded the deal with the farmer when police officers arrived. The police had been following a "Sunrise" crew and had turned up to talk to the farmer. Both sides tried to persuade him: "Sunrise" to let them hold the party and the police to stop it. In the end, "Sunrise" won and the police had to leave. This was private property and it was being leased out for a private party. Sunrise had sold seventeen thousand tickets and they weren't going to let anything sour their event. The local Chief Superintendent, Pauline Coulthard, said afterward, *"There is nothing we can do. Parliament should change the law."*

The next morning, *The Sun* newspaper cried out, *"Don't the police care about enforcing the law of the land? Are they not troubled about what is happening to our young people? Just when will they decide to smash the evil drug pushers in our midst? Only when the drug habit has spread to all of Britain? When the party stretches from shore to shore?"*

But it was already too late – the party almost did stretch from shore to shore. Ecstasy had crept up on Britain and had caught the authorities unaware. By the time they had realized that something big was happening, Ecstasy had reached out to too many people. The scene was growing by the day and the stakes were getting higher and higher. But as the Sunrise organization raised their game, so did the opposition. Tired of being outwitted on the ground by a bunch of mere partygoers, the police resorted to every tactic from road-blocks and phone bugging to mass detentions.

Anti-youth hysteria began to grow, as did the hunt for the "evil" drug-peddling figures at the epicentre of this party craze. A special anti-rave police group, called the Pay Party Intelligence Unit, was established to monitor the situation. Telephone companies were pressurized into preventing party organizers using their systems, while pirate radio stations that had been broadcasting the locations of raves were raided and shut down.

By the end of the summer of 1989, the main rave organizations, "Sunrise", "Biology" and "Energy", had been joined by scores of others. Clubbers coming out of London clubs at that time can testify to the fact that they were regularly assailed by teams of people handing out flyers publicizing the huge variety of raves to choose from. One organization trumped the police by putting on their flyers that the first five thousand people who turned up at their gig would get in free – within a few hours there were more than twenty thousand people dancing in a Surrey field!

On October 1, 1989, three of the previous summer's rave anthems, "Ride On Time", "Pump Up the Jam" and "If Only I Could", were at numbers one, two and three in the national pop charts. Rave culture could no longer be deemed simply as deviant – there were far too many people enjoying it and involved in it. By the end of 1989, the Customs and Excise service were reporting record seizures of Ecstasy and other dance drugs. Customs chief, Douglas Tweddle, explained the increase

ACID HOUSE – BIRTH OF THE RAVE NATION

as the result of *"the rapid rise in popularity of Acid House parties."*

One of the more unsavoury consequences of the success of rave culture was the steadily increasing interest that organized crime was taking in the business. Criminals with record sheets as long as their arms were muscling in on the pay party scene. Hard men were getting involved, putting in their own security and running off with the takings or publicizing fake parties and making off with the door receipts.

In the end, this was what pushed the authorities into action – the fear of crime syndicates accumulating enormous economic power and influence. Raves had now become a serious law and order issue – not just a deviant youth culture that needed cutting down to size.

FREEDOM TO PARTY

Realizing that the Home Secretary was about to announce tough new measures to clamp down on raves, Colston-Hayter launched the Freedom to Party campaign. The campaign concentrated on the licensing law. In Europe, clubbers could quite legally dance all night. In the UK, with its ancient legislation dating back to Lloyd George's Defence of the Realm Act, fun-loving youth were being pushed beyond the law and into the arms of criminals, as soon criminals would be the only ones willing to stage a party after the Government had brought in stricter rules.

The job of putting a Private Members Bill through the House of Commons was given to Graham Bright MP. He had long been a faithful servant of Home Office Ministers and had previously been responsible for the Video Recordings Act against "video nasties". His Entertainment (Increased Penalties) Bill would not create a new criminal offence or give the authorities more power but, as its name suggested, would simply increase the maximum fines payable for unlicensed parties from £2000 to £20,000 and six months' imprisonment. The Labour Party didn't offer any serious opposition to the Bill, so its passage through the house was relatively smooth. To compound matters, Home Office Minister John Patten made it known that he proposed to put into practice an order under the 1988 Criminal Justice Act for confiscation of "criminal proceeds" from illegal parties. He called for the Bill to be rushed through before the next summer.

The Freedom to Party organization felt it had to do something and so fell back on the tried and tested method of holding a public rally to protest against the Bill. The first rally was held in Trafalgar Square in January 1990. A few thousand gathered to listen to speeches and singing. People didn't seem very enthusiastic about the whole thing. The second Freedom to Party rally was held the following March and reflected how low spirits had fallen during the winter. A mere one thousand people marched half-heartedly from Hyde Park. The Freedom to Party campaign rolled on with little hope of victory.

In the same month that the second Freedom to Party rally was being held, Graham Bright's Bill received its second reading in the House. There was a five-hour debate over the Bill, during which MPs spoke about the "evil of Ecstasy" at raves and how British youth were being corrupted. There was little opposition to the bill and so in July 1990, the Entertainment (Increased Penalties) Bill received royal assent and the profit confiscation measures were also enacted. The police, who were now on a high, immediately went on a spree. They arrested 836 ravers at a warehouse party in Leeds, filling the cells in thirty different police stations across West Yorkshire. Only eight people out of all those arrested were subsequently charged.

COMPROMISE CULTURE

Although legislation had been brought in to try to curb large warehouse parties, rave culture wasn't going to disappear overnight. It slowly began to dawn on the police that this was not just yet another passing fancy. If anything, they found that the trend was continuing to grow. The police's Pay Party Intelligence Unit could not expand its size and activities to match that of rave culture – so it was clear that there had to be a compromise.

By the end of 1990, a handful of central London clubs had been granted licenses to stay open after 3am and one was even allowed to stay open for twenty-four hours. The liberalization of the licensing laws, which soon spread throughout the country, didn't happen by chance. The police authorities could not afford to continue to hold huge policing operations weekend after weekend simply to stop young people having parties. As well as the financial strain, they did not have the staff to become full-time party poopers – they had far more important things to be getting on with. Their two-pronged

CRITICAL MASS OUTSIDE A LONDON NIGHTCLUB

assault – cracking down on illegal raves while allowing night-clubs to stay open much longer – was intended to undermine the basis of the rave scene. Slowly, raves became integrated into the existing entertainment infrastructure, the partygoers were brought back into licensed premises and in this way the size of the parties could be contained.

Many saw this era as a time when the rave scene capitulated to the authorities – but in essence it was only the beginning. The Government and the police had to liberalize the UK's archaic licensing laws to accommodate young people, who were no longer satisfied with getting drunk in a pub and stumbling home at closing time. To avoid conflict, the Government had no choice but to go with the new flow or break under the sheer weight of opposition.

RAVE POLITICS

During the late 1970s and early 1980s, the number of disaffected middle-class drop-outs choosing to live a nomadic existence in the UK, travelling in buses and caravans, increased dramatically. These travellers were following a path that had already been cleared for them by hippies and the hippie culture. They were not economic refugees initially, but rather people who rejected city living, materialism and the trappings of a consumer society. They came to be known collectively as the Peace Convoy when, in 1982, they drove to the US air force base at Greenham Common to join members of an anti-nuclear protest camp. They had just attended the annual "People's Free Festival" at Stonehenge, which was the high point of the travellers' year. They returned in 1983 and 1984, by which time, bolstered by curious visitors from the cities, numbers attending had swelled to almost fifty thousand.

Although no one knew it at the time, 1984 would be the last true "People's Free Festival" at Stonehenge. In June 1985, a convoy of 140 vehicles making its way to Stonehenge was halted at a police road-block and moved into a nearby field by a force of one thousand police officers. English Heritage, the administrators of Stonehenge, had taken out an injunction to prohibit that year's festival and had erected barbed wire fencing all around the site. The festival was not going to be allowed to go ahead.

The Assistant Chief Constable of Wiltshire, Lionel Grundy, refused to negotiate an alternative site for the travellers and ordered his men to break up the convoy. It was claimed that as travellers scattered into a nearby bean field, police with helmets and riot gear chased the buses, smashed up their contents and assaulted their occupants. Hundreds of arrests and a long summer of evictions, harassment and vilification in the press followed the destruction. The events of June 1985 came to be known as the "Battle of the Beanfield".

The travellers, previously seen as quaint English eccentrics or, at worst, relatively harmless pastoral anarchists, had now become fully-fledged folk demons. It had been easy to demonize this group of people because they were unconventional and didn't conform to the establishment's idea of model citizens. With the help of an indiscriminate press that dubbed travellers as feckless and dangerous druggies, the Government began to do what it could to make life uncomfortable for the travellers. The 1986 Public Order Act incorporated a section specifically aimed at preventing convoys from massing together. This was the first of many attempts to make an itinerant existence impossible.

In spite of the actions of the Government, the movement grew. The original idealists were now being joined by a new generation: post-punk city squatters whose marginal urban life had been made unbearable by the restrictions they felt had been placed on them by the Conservative Government. Many of them, dressed in ragged black combat gear with haircuts that were reminiscent of punk and Rasta styles – began to join the travellers on the road. By the end of the 1980s, many travellers were highly politicized. Their chosen path had already put them into conflict with landowners and therefore with the Government and the police.

Since the Battle of the Beanfield and the demise of the Stonehenge festival, Glastonbury Festival has become a more important stop-off point on the traveller's annual circuit, a place for them to trade their wares and to party. In 1990, an alliance began to form between travellers and ravers. The travellers had the sites and the know-how to staff and run an event that would last for days rather than hours; the ravers had the sounds and the seductive new synthetic, Ecstasy. Ideological and sartorial differences abounded, but both groups shared an interest in getting high and dancing all night. Ecstasy also allowed two quite different groups to get together to find common cause.

Falling one month before Graham Bright's Bill outlawing unlicensed raves was passed, "Glastonbury 1990" was perfectly placed to capitalize on the growing disaffection felt toward the changes being imposed on the rave scene. While legal action was being taken against one part of the scene, the creative energy was breaking out elsewhere, infusing a new group of people and bringing previously unconnected sectors of society together. Phone numbers were swapped, partnerships formed and two generations of adepts seemed to join hands.

Although the drug culture of the 1960s and that of the 1990s both typified fundamental social changes, the model representatives of each culture could not have been more different, socially, culturally or economically. The "psychedelic scene" of the 1960s was instigated by intellectuals – professors, poets, writers and artists – against the backdrop of the civil rights and anti-Vietnam War movements. The Acid House scene, on the other hand, was conceived in the working class suburbs of Britain by clubbers, football supporters, DJs and a few bohemians in an increasingly harsh economic and social environment with widespread disaffection toward politics.

Drug taking in the 1980s had lost the politicized intellectual context it had in the 1960s; now it was more about hedonism than mind-expansion. The way Acid House developed reflected the UK in the 1980s and not the USA in the 1960s. It was strongly rooted in the traditions of the British youth culture – borrowing liberally from the speed-fuelled Northern Soul all-nighters, the sound systems and warehouse parties of the funk and reggae scenes and the DIY ethics of punk – not those of American counterculture.

STATE OF RAVE

Little notice was taken of this new alliance between travellers and ravers by the youth media or the mainstream press. The police, on the other hand, were well aware of what was happening – they had been collecting information on all these groups from the first day the Pay Party Intelligence Unit had been set up. In May 1992, people began to gather at Castlemorton Common in the Malvern Hills for a huge outdoor rave. The police decided to hold back and let them all congregate in one compact area.

Within a few hours, the Common was transformed into a fully functioning republic under the control of its own citizens; a tiny liberated zone with its own electricity, lighting, housing, catering and leisure facilities – including Ecstasy. All it needed was a bustling population. Local residents, shocked by what was happening in their own back yard, went to the media to bemoan their fate. Dedicated ravers now knew exactly where to go – the gig could not have been better advertised. Soon, cars began to flood into the common and the revelry began. You could dance to the fierce beat of the sound systems as they played for nearly one hundred hours without pause, you could take in street theatre or circus acts, eat at cafes, splash about in the lake, purchase and freely enjoy the drugs of your choice and then, perhaps, rest for a while before starting all over again. This was the twenty-four hour independent "State of Rave".

As Castlemorton slowly wound down, there were stories about local residents, incensed at police inaction, forming vigilante groups to burn the ravers and travellers out. Nearby homeowners were freaking out: *"There's something hypnotic about the continuous pounding beat of the music, and it's driving people living in the front line into a frenzy."* Tabloid newspaper reporters visited the traveller's sites, talked to them, enjoyed their hospitality and then wrote articles about "stoned mothers allowing their dirty children to run wild". Conservative newspapers screamed about the state benefits paid to these "ne'er-do-wells". Ministers promised to take action.

As the revellers left Castlemorton, the police tracked some of the convoys – including the Spiral Tribe – and then moved in to arrest them. Spiral Tribe started out as a small sound system that organized and promoted free parties. Over the years, the group had grown to encompass others who believed in the same ethos. The police impounded the Tribe's vehicles, as well as all their sound and light equipment. They had nothing left – but they weren't going to skulk away. They began a sit-in picket outside Worcester police station that lasted over a week, bolstered by local sympathizers who brought them food and bedding.

THE BACKLASH

At the 1992 Conservative Party Conference, John Major targeted travellers in his keynote speech: *"New age travellers. Not in this age. Not in any age."* This was an unambiguous broadside aimed at the travelling community, warning them that the harassment was not going to stop. The intent was clear – prevent large gatherings. No more Castlemoretons.

Within the loose structure of the free-party/festival/rave alliance, there were differing opinions as to why the pressure was being applied so heavily. Some thought that a Government that was still in shock over the Poll Tax riots of 1990 had understandably become nervous at the creation of a politicized underclass and the potential for an instant mass take-over of a rural area. Some felt it was simply a knee-jerk reaction to a new drug culture. Others felt that this was a Government strategy to have more control over Britons' lifestyles and bring about a gradual reduction in their civil liberties.

Although this sounds like pure paranoia now, to those who had borne the brunt of Conservative rule for nearly a decade and a half, and particularly those travellers who had lived through the Battle of the Beanfield and the subsequent harassment, this was the only way to view the situation. The Poll Tax riots of 1990 were proof enough of a trend that the Government did not wish to see spread.

The strictures against unlicensed raves, festivals and travellers were bound up with other proposed legislation: to criminalize trespass and squatting, to tie down hunt saboteurs, and to remove the right to silence after arrest, as the 1994 Criminal Justice and Public Order Bill proposed. The main aims of this Bill, which senior police officers described as "ill-advised" and civil liberties groups described as "oppressive", seemed to be to strengthen the property rights of landowners, to quell dissenters, to usher members of the rave scene back into the restrictive framework of licensed parties and to prohibit any form of lifestyle that didn't fit in with the Conservative world-view.

As with its policy on drugs, the Government seemed to be using the criminal law to deal with social issues. The president of the Association of Chief Police Officers (ACPO) pointed out at the time that the effect of the Criminal Justice Bill (CJB) would be to *"increase the police's enforcement role by criminalizing issues previously regarded as subject to civil law enforcement procedures or even*

THE POLL TAX RIOTS HIT THE HEADLINES

matters of conscience." The criminalization of the act of trespassing on someone else's property had potentially huge repercussions for anyone who wished to register a protest of any kind.

The Bill also defined and proposed to outlaw a particular genre of music, House, when played in certain circumstances. It stated that *"'music' is defined as sounds wholly or predominantly characterized by the emission of a succession of repetitive beats"* and for the first time the word "rave" appeared in UK legislation. Although other youth movements had inspired new legislation, never before had a government considered young people's music to be so subversive as to require prohibition. It seemed quite obvious to many that the Conservative establishment did not consider dance-drug culture as powerless, meaningless or apolitical.

After 15 years of Conservative rule, the political scene in the United Kingdom had changed beyond recognition. As John Major's Government, in the eyes of some, sought to establish hegemony over all aspects of the political sphere, hundreds of thousands of voters felt that they had became disenfranchized by not registering to vote through fear of being hounded for Poll Tax payments. There was an all-pervasive disillusionment with a political system that seemed to have failed.

This formed the backdrop to the rise of a new era of political protest involving small *ad hoc* organizations. These were mainly action campaigns largely based around environmental issues. These groups preferred the strategies of direct action and mutual collaboration and showed an astute sense of what was required to make a protest dramatic, newsworthy and – most importantly – fun. Under their influence, fears about ecological damage became part of an unstructured cultural movement that was as concerned with social values and responsibility as it was about saving tigers or the rainforests.

Yet the growing politicization of the free-party network increasingly distanced it from the club scene that was meanwhile becoming more mainstream and institutionalized after the Bright Bill. Many clubbers perceived the Criminal Justice Bill as an attack on their own culture and generation. In the early months of 1994, the anti-CJB movement grew. Protest groups mushroomed at an amazing rate. Three mass marches were organized against the CJB in 1994, mostly attended by students, ravers, travellers and others who believed the Bill posed a threat to their social freedoms.

The first march went off without any incident. The second and third marches ended in violent clashes between police and demonstrators. Riot police and mounted police were used against the protesters. Police Chiefs said that the same hard core of rabble-rousers that had been responsible for the Poll Tax riots had caused these riots.

The authorities did not want to countenance, even for a moment, that ordinary people might have legitimate concerns about the proposed legislation.

On November 3, 1994, the Criminal Justice and Public Order Act 1994 was given royal assent and became law. Unlike in the aftermath of the Bright Bill, there were no mass arrests. The police thought that the protesters had resigned themselves to reality. But that was far from the truth. A few hours after the Act was passed, a group of five protesters dodged the House of Common's security and shinned up the drain pipes to its roof, unfurling banners that read "Defy the CJA". They then settled down to set up their own Houses of Parliament and smoke a joint!

The new police powers under the Criminal Justice Act were largely discretionary. Police forces could choose whether to use these powers or not. Eighteen months after the Act was passed, it was estimated that over a thousand people had been arrested under its provisions.

RAVE NEW BUSINESS

By 1993, the rave business was said to be worth at least £2 billion a year and growing – with a million youngsters between them spending £35 million every week. This calculation was based on an average admission charge of £15 and an assumption that the same amount was being spent on drugs. But there was more to rave than mere money. Ecstasy informed just about every aspect of what has latterly been dubbed "ecstasy culture". This attitude slowly started filtering into television advertising for brands such as Tango, Skol and Golden Wonder, and also into chart music, high street fashion, lifestyle magazines, television graphics and even backing music. The Ecstasy cult, which only a few years ago was attracting the venom of the authorities and the bile of the British tabloid press, was now responsible for refreshing the very same media; the old story of youth condemned and then appropriated. After more than a decade of development, rave culture now became a legitimate and lucrative arm of the leisure industry, affecting highly commercialized venues such as the Ministry of Sound and Cream, as well as glossy magazines, record labels and merchandizing.

ESSENTIAL ECSTASY READING

Like every other sphere that was influenced by Ecstasy culture, book publishing did not escape untouched. The financial potential of the new club and drug culture was too much of a temptation to miss. Ecstasy creations began to flood the market, from pulp fiction "drugsploitation" and DJ profiles to self-published books that were pushed out cheaply and quickly.

One of the key tracts published about this era is the incisive *Ecstasy and Dance Culture*. The author, Nicholas Saunders, had already written *Alternative London*, a guide to fringe pursuits in the Capital. Saunders was a throw-back to the 1960s, whose enthusiasm for Ecstasy bordered on the evangelical. An earnest, balding, fifty-odd year-old, he had fallen in love with Ecstasy in the 1980s and was worried by what he considered the negative press that Ecstasy was attracting. He was hardly a typical E-head, but he was distressed at the demonization of Ecstasy.

In 1992, Saunders called a meeting in London's Covent Garden, under the banner "Positive Aspects of MDMA", and obsessively began to collect all the information he could about Ecstasy. He published this data in book form from his own studio in Covent Garden. It appeared as a trilogy – *E for Ecstasy, Ecstasy and the Dance Culture* and *Ecstasy Reconsidered* – all of which became underground success stories. Saunders wanted to combat what he saw as misinformation, given that he was trying to spread the good word about the drug's therapeutic potential.

DANCE FLOOR ECSTASY

Saunders was tireless in his work. He published monthly tests of the chemicals in Ecstasy pills and visited drug researchers all over the world reporting back on their work. He took his writing very seriously. Rather than offer trite slogans, he gave out statistics and reports and aimed for gentle persuasion. Saunders wasn't much like Timothy Leary, but he was just as enthusiastic about his drug as Leary had been about LSD. The high regard in which he was held by some clubbers and users of Ecstasy was an indication of just how eager people were to acquire more knowledge about this drug.

In his first two books, *E for Ecstasy*, and *Ecstasy and the Dance Culture*, Saunders suggests that, as well as enlivening and enriching dance culture, the drug can improve sexual and family relationships, cure chronic depression, improve problem-solving, increase physical fitness, advance sporting prowess, relieve pain and even lead to better job prospects!

In the last book, *Ecstasy Reconsidered*, as the title suggests Saunders looked again at Ecstasy, except this time he was concentrating on the "down" side. For this, at least, he must be given some credit, as most drug gurus don't even countenance the fact that their favourite substances might have a negative aspect. After his research, Saunders felt he was still of the opinion that Ecstasy had a great deal that was positive about it and could be used very productively.

THE IRVINE WELSH PHENOMENON

As literary phenomenona go – Irvine Welsh was the brightest star of the British writing firmament in the 1990s. Brought up on a housing estate in Scotland, Welsh spent many years drifting in and out of heroin addiction. In 1993, almost completely out of the blue, he presented the reading public with *Trainspotting*, a crazy narrative following the fortunes of a group of Edinburgh youths: junkies, people with AIDS, ravers and boozers. This exceptional book from an unknown writer sold half a million copies in just three years and its film treatment has gone on to become one of the most popular British movies of the 1990s.

Trainspotting was the cult text of the decade, not just because it is written so well, but because the writing and the characters rang true to anyone who had really been immersed in drug culture. Welsh managed to bring to the fore the way a drug-taker thinks, feels and acts and he managed to get across to readers the very real chaotic nature of their lives. As he said in the foreword of his play script for *Trainspotting*, *"other realities exist, have to be shown to exist."* This humanizing of the drug-user or addict went a long way toward overturning stereotypes and demonic images. Of course, the book spawned a million debates about whether it was glamorizing drug taking, but none dampened its popularity.

So, with the phenomenal success of *Trainspotting*, Welsh moved from relative obscurity to the very centre of British writing. With his next books, Welsh explored the social and emotional outlines of the British club scene. *Ecstasy*, a collection of stories, seemed primarily concerned with Britain's decay and the growing demand for social conformity. The three stories – or "chemical romances" – explore the part that the drug plays in the lives of the three main characters. This book brought him attention from a hitherto non-book reading sector of the population. Some Ecstasy evangelists bought the book simply because of its title! Even when he doesn't get it exactly right, Welsh manages to come up with some effortlessly readable prose that captures the prevailing mood – and this is, perhaps, his enduring appeal.

Welsh aptly summarized the inherent dichotomy of the Ecstasy scene in the UK during an interview he gave for *i-D* magazine in 1996: *"Is it a big shattering New Age thing? Or is it just a more sophisticated way to get off your tits and have a good time?"* The spiritual trippers saw Ecstasy as a sacrament and the rave heads just saw it as a good-time pill. This was proletarian hedonism through and through and Welsh managed to capture it perfectly. As one of the characters in his book *Ecstasy* suggests, it was almost their *duty* to party, to prove to themselves that despite everything, they were still alive!

JUNGLE BEAT

The common musical theme unravelled as the original Chicago house has gone through a hundred different mutations – Garage, Techno, Belgian New Beat, Hardcore Techno, Ragga, and by way of some kind of respite, Trance and Ambient music. A drop in tempo can quickly bring an Ecstasy-user down from his or her trip. So, if Ecstasy and dancing were to change the world, those who spread the psychedelic message needed DJs who were going to be able to maintain a continuity of rhythm and tempo throughout the night, so that nothing would interrupt or interfere with a clubber's Ecstasy high.

The demand for continual repetitive House music throughout the 1990s meant that Ecstasy soon became the most important ingredient of a typical night out. The growing status of both the DJ and Ecstasy also increased the importance of the "DJ remix", a version of the dance track that emphasized beats exactly on the bar – to facilitate seamless switching between records. As more and more Ecstasy was consumed, the demand for different kinds of Ecstasy-inspired music grew. Eventually, the supply would grow to match.

The musical genre that almost single-handedly saved dance music from

Ecstasy-related stagnation in the UK is Jungle, otherwise known as "drum and bass". This music consists of a frenetic percussion track at almost 320 beats per minute, a second percussion track and an irregular, shifting bass line. Jungle relies upon speeded-up break beats with vocals, strings and synthesized sounds sandwiched between the percussion and bass. This genre seemed to have rejected the totally repetitive 4/4 basis of most House and Techno music.

Break beat is generally accepted to have originated in the Bronx, New York, in the early 1970s. Jungle takes these break beats and, with the help of technology, digitally breaks them up. There is no House-like repetition at the heart of Jungle music, instead there are almost non-stop circles of change and difference. Jungle's manic percussion is widely considered to reflect, or arise from, the frenetic pace of inner-city life.

This emphasis on fast urban lifestyles is also combined with an emphasis on "darkness", which underlines the shadow cast by inner-city poverty in which many Jungle consumers find themselves as well as the largely black origins of Jungle music. There is no suggestion in Jungle music that societal change is imminent or that Ecstasy is going to change the world. Jungle's sense of darkness would seem to suggest that the Acid House generation in the UK had finally grown up.

GOING GLOBAL ON E

Inevitably, as time went on, the rave scene broke down into genres and sub-genres in the UK, but not before it had been successfully exported world-wide. The Netherlands has a well-established rave scene, in which drug users receive some protection from the uncertainties of the illicit drug market through a drug-testing service available outside the clubs, provided by drug agencies. This service tests the purity of any drug that a user has bought and advises whether it is worth taking. In addition, there are personal testing kits that users can buy to carry out their own checks at home. These testing kits are now also available in the UK.

Rave culture has made inroads into much of Europe – including Scandinavia, despite the Nordic country's zero-tolerance approach to drugs. Even the Chinese are raving on E; in the late 1990s, the police there made their first seizures of Ecstasy – or "head rocking drug", as it is called in the country. Chinese police have been told to stop anyone wearing shades on suspicion of being a drug user! In an ironic turnaround, Asia and the Far East, source of most of the world's heroin, is now being flooded with European Ecstasy cooked up in make-shift laboratories by European chemists. Ecstasy is the top drug for young people in Indonesia, where, for some reason, it's called Bon Jovi!

CHANGE OF TACK

One of the more interesting outcomes of the proliferation of drug use is that Government and other authorities have been forced to take a more pragmatic view of young people and their use of drugs. This is well illustrated by what happened when the Merseyside Regional Drug Information Service (MRDIS) published its *Chill-Out* leaflet in 1992 – one of the earliest pieces of health and safety information about drugs and raves. There were front-page banner headlines in the tabloid newspapers to the effect that parents and the moral guardians of society should go round to the agency and throw the author of the leaflet into the river. The organisation's funding was also put in jeopardy.

Within months, however, the same advice was appearing in the established medical press and was very quickly being taken up by the Government in its drug advice campaign. No longer was the Government only pushing a "Just Say No" stance on drugs. Governmental agencies had to come to terms with the fact that young people were using drugs and so someone needed to advise them in a non-judgemental manner about how to look after themselves. This was a far cry from Government policy in the 1970s and 1980s when the only drug literature available was the kind that demonized and criminalized all drugs and drug users.

This change affected club owners too, many of whom were now taking on board the health and safety issues around drugs, following guidelines and allowing drug agency workers on to their premises to help, offer advice and act as paramedics for anyone who might be in trouble.

SLIPPERY SLOPE

Just as LSD brought together a nation of "heads" in the 1960s and 1970s, Ecstasy was central to the rave phenomenon because it delivered dance energy, which in turn united fans in some kind of shared, collective ritual. Again, just like its predecessor LSD and contrary to what the evangelists had preached, Ecstasy didn't change the whole world. What it did do was turn hedonism into a ritual, creating a form of music whose sole purpose was to increase the chemical and spiritual high. With some ravers now taking up to twenty pills in one weekend, something had to give. The "loved-up" feeling of the early Ecstasy days has now disappeared only to be replaced by a harder-edged sound and atmosphere. Just as the democratization of the acid trip led to a coarsening and disentangling of that first psychedelic scene, so rave was ultimately beset by bad drugs, bad undercurrents, and even a few dance-floor deaths.

A BITTER PILL

In the early hours of the morning of November 12, 1995, in the Essex village of Latchingdon, England, a young woman was very sick and very scared. Her pupils were dilated and her head was throbbing. She screamed for help and then collapsed unconscious. This was Leah Betts who, only a few hours earlier, had taken an Ecstasy pill with her best friend Sarah Cargill. The previous day had been Leah's eighteenth birthday and she had been holding a party at her home. Her father Paul, a former police officer, and her stepmother, Janet, a volunteer anti-drugs worker, were there to make sure that everyone had a good time and that the party did not get out of hand.

At about 8 o'clock that evening, Leah and Sarah went downstairs to join the other guests. Only fifteen minutes earlier, the two girls had taken an Ecstasy tablet each and were all set for an evening of fun. Leah cut her birthday cake, had a few drinks, danced with her friends and seemed to be enjoying herself. Just after midnight, she ran upstairs to the bathroom and was violently sick. Scared, she called out for her parents and then fell into a coma from which she never woke up. Paul and Janet had no idea what was happening to their daughter until Sarah told them what Leah had taken.

Leah was taken to the Broomfield Hospital in Chelmsford and put on a ventilator. She remained in a coma for a week while her parents struggled to make sense of what had happened to their daughter. After carrying out a series of brain scans, the doctors told Paul and Janet that there was severe cerebral swelling and all they could do was wait to see whether the swelling would go down and Leah come out of her coma.

While Leah was in hospital, the tabloid media got hold of the story and dramatized the saga in huge front-page headlines. Day after day, while her parents tried to come to the difficult decision of whether or not to switch off Leah's life support system, the story steadily grew.

Before the event, nobody would have believed that something like this could have happened. After all, Leah was a young, white, affluent college student, an English Rose who lived in a sleepy village in the heart of the Conservative heartland of south-east England – a genuine daughter of Middle England. She was any kid. She was not from a sink estate in Scotland, or a sleazy area of a big city like London or Manchester. This was a perfect story for the tabloids – they couldn't have invented a better one if they had tried. It inspired the most hysterical and sustained drug panic of the 1990s. Every day, the tabloid newspapers published huge pictures of the comatose Leah on her deathbed in the hospital. They launched "war on drugs" campaigns and even endorsed phone lines by which people could "shop a dealer". Many of them sent out reporters to find the "murderers" who had supplied the Ecstasy pill in the first place – omitting to tell their readers that it was Leah's best friend who had actually got hold of the pill for her and was therefore technically guilty of the crime.

On November 15, doctors told the family that Leah was brain dead and on the 16th Leah's life support system was switched off. But Leah's death did nothing to cool the tabloid frenzy – but actually intensified it. Leah's parents were just as determined as the newspapers that their daughter's death would be used as an anti-drugs lesson, allowing a video of her funeral to be distributed to schools and her face to be featured on a nation-wide billboard campaign.

The huge posters were an eerie sight. Each one showed a photograph of a smiling Leah, shoulder-length hair thrown back, framed in a black border with a single word writ large: "Sorted". Under that image was the grim warning: "Just one Ecstasy tablet took Leah

"Sorted" – tablet from the same batch as the one Leah Betts took

Betts". These posters were plastered on more than a thousand billboards all round the country. Leah Betts had, in death, become Ecstasy culture's first idol, more famous than she could ever have imagined. She had become a dual symbol. To parents she was a symbol of innocence defiled and lost, to the younger generation she was a symbol of the huge gap in understanding between the generations.

But Leah Betts did one very important service to British society – she changed forever the stereotypical image of a drug taker. People who had spent a great deal of time over the years sensationalizing the issue and demonizing drug-takers, suddenly realized that these drug-takers were their own sons and daughters. *The Sunday Times* newspaper put it like this: *"Leah always told her mother and father she was appalled by drugs. But perhaps like so many youngsters, she did not see Ecstasy as a drug at all."*

Polite society was shocked and scandalized – it was as if their children had suddenly turned into Martians. Parents came across a culture in their midst that was so alien to them they found it hard to believe it had existed alongside them all this time. This was a culture within which drugs were good, not bad; normal, not deviant. Newspaper editors who sent reporters out to the nightclubs were astounded to get back reports that educated middle-class people – doctors, engineers, lawyers, journalists, people exactly like themselves – loved Ecstasy and were using it on a regular basis.

The immense volume of coverage that Ecstasy got at that time showed that some nerve, deep in the national psyche, had been touched. Many people previously opposed to harm-reduction strategies, now started to call for them. Middle-class parents were genuinely scared that their beloved children would be criminalized for something that was apparently a widespread phenomenon. *The Independent* went furthest, saying: *"Young people such as Leah Betts need to be protected. The way to do that is to understand what they are consuming and control its quality. That may mean making it a substance whose use is frowned upon, but not criminalized: like smoking or parking on double yellow lines."* Attitudes hadn't voluntarily changed because people were suddenly aware of the extent of Ecstasy consumption in society, but because they realized they had no other choice. Realistically, this thing was not going to go away, as was succinctly put in a *Times* headline: *"Dangers will not make us change our habit, say Ecstasy users."*

While the outside world was struggling to come to terms with all these revelations – the Ecstasy world was also agitated. Why had Leah Betts died? Was it a dodgy tab? Had she drunk too much alcohol on top of her E? Many just didn't believe that MDMA might have been the problem – their reaction was that Leah Betts was a "lightweight", someone who couldn't handle drugs. Those who did believe that Ecstasy might have killed Leah Betts had a very pertinent point to make though, as one user put it, *"There's been plenty of deaths. You just go out and do it the next weekend."* Another explained it this way, *"Alcohol rots your brain and no one stops drinking when someone dies from that. I know the risks and I'm willing to keep on taking them."*

In all the hysteria surrounding Leah Betts' death, one thing had gone past virtually unnoticed. Although the cause of Leah's death was given as "Ecstasy poisoning" at the coroner's inquest, Dr John Henry, scientific adviser to the Government's National Poisons Unit, stated his belief that her death was actually the result of water intoxication: or dilutional hyponatremia. Leah had started to panic when her Ecstasy experience went awry and had drunk enough liquid to kill her. Soon it also became clear that the image of Leah as a first-time Ecstasy user who had died on her first ever trip was also untrue – she had certainly taken the drug before.

The local police poured huge resources into finding the dealers who had sold the drug to Leah Betts. The investigation lasted over a year – but after a hugely expensive prosecution, the only people who were convicted were three teenagers – her friends. One of them was given a conditional discharge and the other two were cautioned. The trials revealed a new world to British society. A new, but very ordinary world, where many thousands of petty drug deals are done every weekend. A youngster buys some pills and hands them out to his or her mates. None of them considered themselves drug dealers or criminals. So the "evil dealer" was a college friend and the "murderer" was the best friend.

When it became known that the real reason for Leah's death was that she had drunk too much water, journalists took very little notice. Dr Henry is less dismissive of the truth. After all, the majority of Ecstasy-related deaths have been associated with dehydration and a common myth that circulated on the club scene was that lots of water is an antidote to the chemical effects of the drug. Dr Henry is well aware that this kind of myth can lead to the death of more people like Leah Betts. Some drug education experts have argued that Leah's death was likely to have resulted from misinformation and that misinformation is the greater danger.

ONE STEP OVER THE LINE

In January 1997, a pop star called Brian Harvey, lead singer of London boy-band E17, stirred things up for himself when he gave an interview saying that Ecstasy can make you a better person. That, in itself, might have gone unnoticed – it was slightly cheeky but relatively

BRIAN HARVEY – INVITING A PUBLIC OUTCRY

uncontroversial. Unfortunately, in the same interview, he also confessed to once having taken 12 Ecstasy pills in one go without any problems – and then driving home!

This admission prompted an amazing response – even the Prime Minister, John Major, mentioned it in Parliament. Newspapers, television, radio – everybody seemed to be astonished and shocked and scandalized by this admission from the pop star. There followed various sensationalist articles, including a five-page spread in the *Daily Mirror*, all about the horrors of Ecstasy. The *Mirror*'s spread was ringed with oval shaped portraits of victims of the "killer" Ecstasy. The ubiquitous name of Leah Betts was in the headlines yet again and all sorts of clubs were suddenly in imminent danger of being shut down. Seventeen different radio stations announced that they were putting into effect an immediate ban on E17 records – effectively killing off any possible success their new single – just out – might have had. Last, but not least, Brian Harvey was thrown out of his band.

Many young people, including Ecstasy users, were amazed that anyone would admit to taking 12 Ecstasy pills in one go, but they were more shocked by the reaction that this admission received. Most of them were quite relieved that someone had spoken out publicly about something that was happening every weekend, in every club, right across the country. Ecstasy was such a common phenomenon by now that most young people were just amused by Brian Harvey's comments. The popular Radio 4 morning current affairs programme *Today* interviewed some young clubbers, who all agreed with the general sentiments that Brian Harvey had voiced about the drug. Many of them said they hated his music but thought he made sense when he spoke about what Ecstasy does for people.

What was fascinating about the reaction from the establishment, on the other hand, was that it came at a time when the seemingly inexorable rise of Ecstasy on the club scene was actually beginning to slow down – for the first time in a decade.

ECSTASY AND APARTHEID

Not all drug scandals involve the death or overdose of an individual. If the United States Government was willing to spend many millions of dollars experimenting with psychoactive substances to determine whether they might be of use in warfare, it is no wonder that other countries thought the same way.

One of the great evils of the twentieth century has been the apartheid system in South Africa. Those that sought to prop up the system used everything from the Bible to social Darwinism to justify their malevolence. They even went down the road of perverting science to fulfil their evil intentions and keep an entire people brutalized in sub-human bondage. It might be a surprise to many who have taken Ecstasy to find that some people think it can be used for reasons other than the therapeutic or pleasurable. But this was just what was happening in South Africa during the early 1990s.

While addressing a hearing of the South African Truth and Reconciliation Commission in Cape Town, Dr Johan Koekemoer, a chemist, revealed that South Africa's apartheid regime had ordered his pharmaceutical research laboratories to make a tonne of Ecstasy for secret riot control. He confessed to running a Government project that made £120 million worth of the drug. He said that, in 1992, he had been told to make 912kgs of Ecstasy as part of a chemical warfare project. Based on a dosage of 125mgs per pill, that's enough Ecstasy for 73 million separate hits!

At the time, he was working for a company called the Roodeplaat Research Laboratory, which was actually a front for army development work. Dr Koekemoer told the Commission that his boss, Dr Philip Mijburgh, who was the overall chief of the secret Delta G facility where Koekemoer worked, said he had received an official order for production of the drug Ecstasy, code-named Baxil, from the Surgeon General. Dr Koekemoer said he was told that it was to be used for incapacitating black protesters, but he had informed his superiors that he didn't believe Ecstasy was a good incapacitator. When they wouldn't listen, he began to suspect that the real reason for the order to produce the drug was that his superiors might be privately dealing in the drug.

The shadowy figure behind Ecstasy production in South Africa was Wouter Basson, former head of army special operations, who is now facing criminal charges for being in possession of Ecstasy. Although the evidence presented at the Commission was that he was ostensibly having Ecstasy manufactured for the purpose of "incapacitating the enemy", word on the ground was that he was producing the drug for international distribution in order to make himself a whole lot of money. Word on the ground also says that Basson still has a great deal of the original 912kgs of Ecstasy hidden away somewhere in South Africa! Local ravers are waiting with bated breath for someone to find Basson's Brownies, as they have come to be known!

THE CHEMICAL GENERATION

At the start of the twenty-first century, it has become evident that some fads and trends will continue. People continue to use a variety of drugs on a recreational or hedonistic basis, despite knowing the potential negative consequences associated with them: Psychoactive drugs have increasingly become very much a part of mainstream society. Social norms have been steadily changing to the point that drugs are not only available, but are much in demand and supplied by a large and organized supply network. Obviously, we live in a world that consists of thrill-seeking and risk-taking individuals who are willing to experiment with a variety of mind-altering compounds.

There are ongoing studies to determine why people use drugs for their pleasure. Currently, social pressure from peers and societal role models remain at the top of the list of reasons why young people take drugs. Some individuals choose to experiment with drugs to satisfy their curiosity about the unknown. Some experimentation with drugs appears to be part of an adolescent "initiation ritual" or "rite of passage". There are also those who use drugs as a pathway for gaining insight, having fun and creating a sense of belonging. All said, people will continue to use drugs, licit or otherwise, to make themselves feel happier.

Although Ecstasy is no longer the shiny new drug it used to be – it is still consumed very widely all over the world. But like all the other drugs that have gone before it, Ecstasy has simply joined the long list of mind-altering substances now on offer for the new twenty-first century drug adepts. Many who will now start to use Ecstasy will have nothing to do with the rave culture and will probably know nothing about Ecstasy's roots. But for all that things have changed, much has remained and will continue to remain the same – not least the ongoing, restless, tireless human search for happiness and contentment through chemistry. The story is not over yet.

INDEX

BIBLIOGRAPHY

Annual Report on the State of the Drugs Problem in the European Union. European Monitoring Centre for Drugs and Drug Addiction, 1998.

Beck, Jerome and Rosenbaum, Marsha, Pursuit of Ecstasy. State University of New York Press, Albany, 1994.

Boy George, with Bright, Spencer, Take It Like A Man. Sidgwick and Jackson, London, 1995.

Cohen, Richard S. The Love Drug: Marching to the Beat of Ecstasy. Haworth Medical Press, 1998.

Collin, Matthew, Altered State: The Story of Ecstasy Culture and Acid House. Serpent's Tail, 1997.

Eisner, Bruce, Ecstasy – The MDMA Story. Ronin Publishing, Berkeley, 1989.

Escohotado, Antonio, A Brief History of Drugs: From the Stone Age to the Stoned Age. Park Street Press, Vermont, 1996.

Gilroy, Paul, There Ain't No Black in the Union Jack. Hutchinson, London, 1987.

Hayes, Gary and Baker, Oswin, Drug Prevalence in the UK: Report to the Department of Health. Institute for the Study of Drug Dependence, 1998.

Melechi, Antonio (ed.), Psychedelia Britannica. Turnaround, 1997.

O'Mahoney, So, Bernard, This is Ecstasy? Mainstream, Edinburgh, 1997.

Robson, Phillip, Forbidden Drugs. Oxford University Press, 1999.

Saunders, Nicholas, Ecstasy and Dance Culture.

Saunders, Nicholas, Ecstasy Reconsidered. Nicholas Saunders, 1997.

Shulgin, Ann and Alexander, PIHKAL. Transform Press, Berkeley, 1991.

39th Session of the Commission on Narcotic Drugs, Amphetamine-type Stimulants: A Global Review. Vienna, 1996.

Tyler, Andrew, Street Drugs. Coronet Paperbacks, 1986.

United Nations Office for Drug Control and Crime Prevention, Global Illicit Drug Trends 1999. UN, New York, 1999.

Welsh, Irvine, Trainspotting. 1993.